For God So Loved the World

John

NELSON

IMPACT™

Bible Study Series

For God So Loved the World

John

NELSON IMPACT
A Division of Thomas Nelson Publishers
Since 1798

www.thomasnelson.com

The publishers are grateful to Michael Christopher for his collaboration, writing skills, and editorial help in developing the content for this book.

Published by Nelson Impact, a Division of Thomas Nelson, Inc., P.O. Box 141000, Nashville, Tennessee 37214.

Printed in the United States of America.

05 06 07 – 9 8 7 6 5 4 3 2 1

A Word from the Publisher…

Be diligent to present yourself approved to God, a worker who does not need to be ashamed, rightly dividing the word of truth.

2 Timothy 2:15 NKJV

We are so glad that you have chosen this study guide to enrich your biblical knowledge and strengthen your walk with God. Inside you will find great information that will deepen your understanding and knowledge of this book of the Bible.

Many tools are included to aid you in your study, including ancient and present-day maps of the Middle East, as well as timelines and charts to help you understand when the book was written and why. You will also benefit from sidebars placed strategically throughout this study guide, designed to give you expanded knowledge of language, theology, culture, and other details regarding the Scripture being studied.

We consider it a joy and a ministry to serve you and teach you through these study guides. May your heart be blessed, your mind expanded, and your spirit lifted as you walk through God's Word.

Blessings,

Edward "Les" Middleton

Edward (Les) Middleton, M. Div.
Editor-in-Chief, Nelson Impact

TIMELINE OF NEW

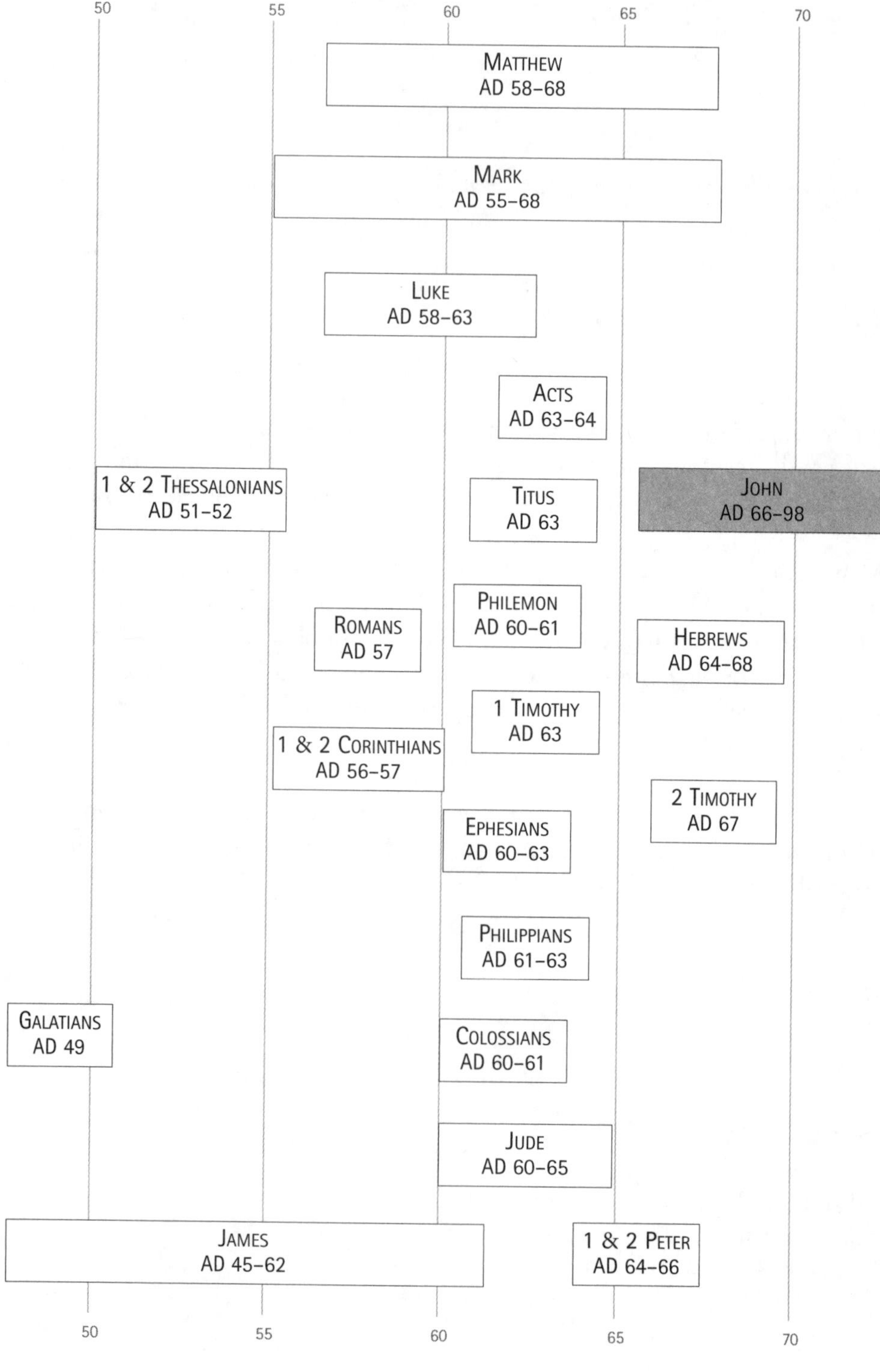

Testament Writings

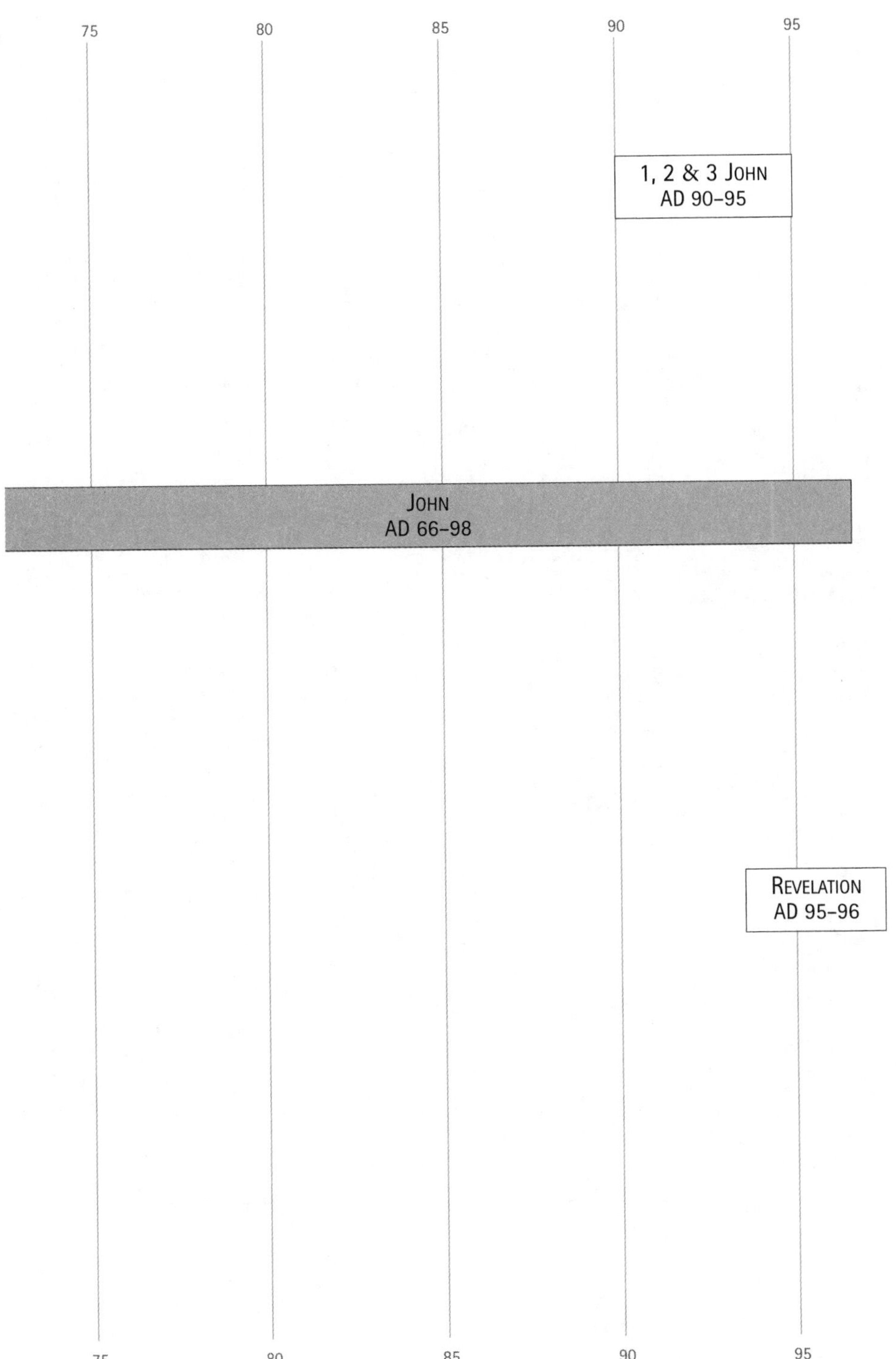

Old Middle East

★ The book of John was written in Ephesus.

Middle East of Today

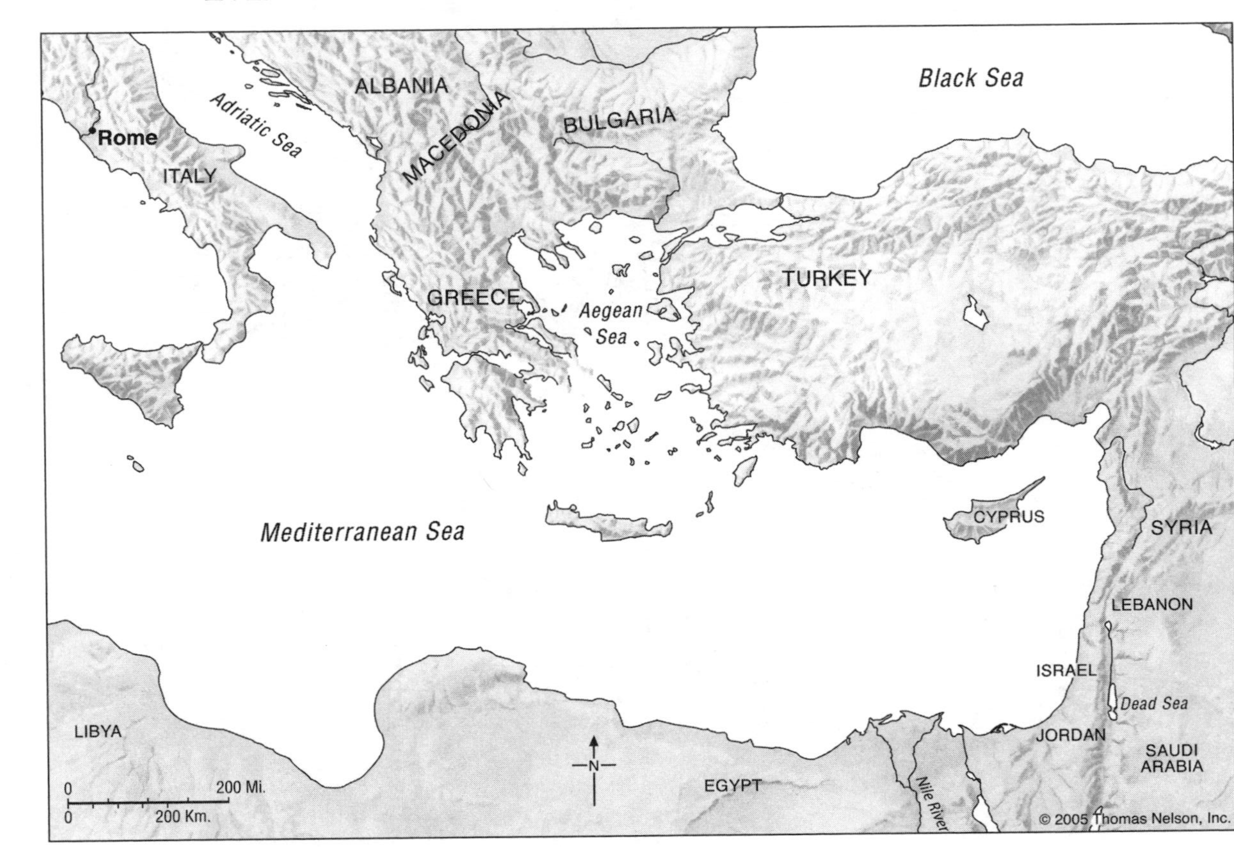

Old Testament Divisions

The Pentateuch

Genesis
Exodus
Leviticus
Numbers
Deuteronomy

Wisdom Literature

Job
Psalms
Proverbs
Ecclesiastes
Song of Solomon

The Historical Books

Joshua
Judges
Ruth
1 Samuel
2 Samuel
1 Kings
2 Kings
1 Chronicles
2 Chronicles
Ezra
Nehemiah
Esther

The Prophetic Books

Isaiah
Jeremiah
Lamentations
Ezekiel
Daniel
Hosea
Joel
Amos
Obadiah
Jonah
Micah
Nahum
Habakkuk
Zephaniah
Haggai
Zechariah
Malachi

New Testament Divisions

The Four Gospels
Matthew
Mark
Luke
John

History
Acts

The Epistles of Paul
Romans
1 Corinthians
2 Corinthians
Galatians
Ephesians
Philippians
Colossians
1 Thessalonians
2 Thessalonians
1 Timothy
2 Timothy
Titus
Philemon

The General Epistles
Hebrews
James
1 Peter
2 Peter
1 John
2 John
3 John
Jude

Apocalyptic Literature
Revelation

Icon Key

Throughout this study guide, you will find many icon sidebars that will aid and enrich your study of this book of the Bible. To help you identify what these icons represent, please refer to the key below.

Biblical Grab Bag

A biblical grab bag full of interesting facts and tidbits.

Bible

Further exploration of biblical principles and interpretations, along with a little food for thought.

Language

Word usages, definitions, interpretations, and information on the Greek and Hebrew languages.

Culture

Customs, traditions, and lifestyle practices in biblical times.

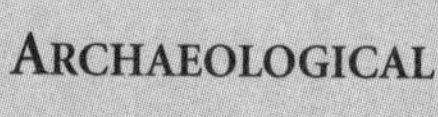

Archaeological

Archaeological discoveries and artifacts that relate to biblical life, as well as modern-day discoveries.

Contents

INTRODUCTION

Over the centuries the Gospel of John has acquired a unique reputation among the sixty-six books of the Bible. It certainly contains a loving portrait of Jesus Christ, but it's probably better known for presenting one of the clearest and most convincing affirmations ever written of His deity as the Son of God.

In fact, only in the book of John does Christ Himself repeat all seven of the well-known "I am" statements of Christianity:

I am . . .
1. The Bread of Life (John 6:35)
2. The Light of the World (John 8:12)
3. The Door of the Sheep (John 10:7)
4. The Good Shepherd (John 10:11, 14)
5. The Resurrection and the Life (John 11:25)
6. The Way and the Truth and the Life (John 14:6)
7. The True Vine (John 15:1)

Beyond that, in a subsection sometimes called the "Book of Signs" (John 2:1–12:50), John details seven miracles (or "signs") that proclaim Jesus as the Messiah. Yet he does not spend a single verse on the classic elements of the other three Gospels—Christ's genealogy, the story of His birth, His baptism (although John does include some interaction with John the Baptist), His temptation, His parables, His casting out of demons, His transfiguration, His agony in the Garden of Gethsemane, or even His ascension into heaven.

On the contrary, John concentrates on Christ's ministry in Jerusalem. In addition to including more information than any other Gospel on the God-ordained feasts of the Jewish nation, John also presents what many consider a far more "personal" Jesus, by including his remembrances of Christ's actual conversations with various individuals, and several of His longer interactions with His disciples. John also includes a number of lengthy discourses that explain the meaning of the seven miracles.

Indeed, John is so selective in what he records that some have wondered whether his methods were *fair* or *valid.* But these are not terms that even apply, for a gospel is not a modern biography, or even a modern history. On the contrary, it is a recounting of the words, the events, and the personal impressions that recorded themselves most indelibly on the minds of the individual writers. That John might have had a more strictly defined purpose in his account makes it no more and no less credible than the others; it just makes it . . . different.

Who Was This Man Named John?

The man we know as John would have been called *Yochanan* (pronounced *yo-ka-non*) by his Hebrew friends and relatives. He and his brother, *Ya'akov* (James), were sons of a fisherman known in English as Zebedee. Both James and John were mending nets on the Sea of Galilee when the two brothers were called as disciples by Christ. On the same day Christ called another set of brothers, Peter and Andrew, also working as fishermen in the same place.

Peter and John soon became perhaps the two best-known of Jesus' twelve disciples. Most of us remember Peter for his straight-ahead, always committed, sometimes impetuous personality. On the other hand, John described himself as "the disciple Jesus loved" four separate times in his own book, indicating that he might have been a favorite of the Master Himself. This could have been true for any number of reasons—even, perhaps, because he required fewer corrections

WHAT IS A "GOSPEL" ANYWAY?

The New Testament begins with the four Gospels—*Matthew, Mark, Luke,* and *John.* All four are first-century AD, largely eyewitness accounts of the life of Jesus Christ. The first three are commonly known as the "synoptic" Gospels because they present the story in very similar ways, from similar viewpoints.

John is the odd man out, not because his story contradicts any of the others, but because he was far more selective in what he reported. And also, as this study guide will make clear, he seemed to be writing for a slightly different purpose, not so much to tell what happened as to explain what it meant.

Despite all this, however, some critics have said that the four Gospels can't be true because they don't all include the same events, or even contain the same details about the ones they do report. But this same argument can be used even more convincingly in favor of their *authenticity.* Rather than being almost identical—as they might be if they were hatched up by a committee and falsified on purpose—each one of the Gospels reflects a slightly different "take" on the same series of events. None contradict any of the others—they just focus on different aspects.

You'd get something very similar if you asked four eyewitnesses to the destruction of the World Trade Center in New York on September 11, 2001, to write down what they saw. Those different versions would enhance one another and fill in different details, from different angles of observation. They would not disprove one another at all. On the contrary, their very *humanity* would enhance their value, for they would *deal with events in terms we can all relate to.*

This is the great strength of the three synoptic Gospels. It is also one of the great strengths of the book of John, except that John is more "different" than all three of the others!

and less energy to deal with than a man of Peter's disposition! It might also be true that John's more peaceful personality (if that's really what he had) was more in sync with that of Christ Himself. More than once the Gospels mention the Savior's occasional, very human need to escape from the crowds and simply rest.

Most commentators believe that John wrote his gospel in the ten-year stretch between AD 85 and AD 95, some fifty or more years after Christ ascended into heaven. Others have suggested an earlier date, based largely on evidence arising from recent archaeological discoveries. However, more conservative scholars continue to insist on the later date, not least because so many believe the book of John was written when its author was an older man. This is based on internal evidence near the end of the book, but cannot be proved conclusively.

WHAT WAS THE FEAST OF DEDICATION?

Among all his other notable firsts, John is the only Gospel writer who mentions the following event:

> Now it was the *Feast of Dedication* in Jerusalem, and it was winter. And Jesus walked in the temple, in Solomon's porch. (John 10:22–23 NKJV italics added)

The *Feast of Dedication* is known in more modern times as *Hanukkah* (or *Chanukah*, or by any of several other spelling variations). Hanukkah was not one of the seven feasts of the Lord ordained by God in the Old Testament (Leviticus, chapter 23). On the contrary, Hanukkah is a traditional Jewish holiday commemorating the rededication of the temple in Jerusalem after its defilement by Antiochus of Syria, which occurred some two hundred years before the birth of Christ.

Most scholars who mention this reference at all do so in connection with the concepts of traditional versus sacred. The message is that Christ did not teach against tradition per se; indeed, He actually honored it when He could. As anyone who has ever seen *Fiddler on the Roof* knows, tradition can be good!

Only when the people of His day substituted the traditions of men in place of the commandments of God, did Christ object.

In truth, the same applies to John's authorship itself. Unlike, for example, the letters of Paul, nowhere in his book does John actually identify himself by name. However, it certainly is possible to build a solid chain of circumstantial evidence from several verses, taken together, which involves a process of logical elimination beyond the scope of this study guide. On the other hand, external evidence for John's authorship is somewhat stronger; it includes both longstanding tradition and the testimony or endorsement of several of the early church fathers.

In terms of its overall purpose, John's Gospel definitely came into being at a time when the early church was still struggling to establish itself and express its founding doctrines. Partly for this reason, perhaps, John focused on recording Jesus' "signs" and their explanations. He seemed to want his readers to come to a clear understanding of both the *divinity* and the *specific teachings* of Christ Himself. Thus he produced what some consider the most evangelistic of the four Gospels, one that has probably been printed separately and passed out to more new believers than any other book of the Bible, including Psalms and Proverbs.

John is also the only book in the Bible that states its own purpose in its author's own words in clear, precise language: ". . . that you may believe that Jesus is the Christ, the Son of God, and that believing you may have life in His name" (John 20:31 NKJV).

Faith vs. Trust

John made one more subtle point that can sometimes fly under the radar. According to one translation, John used the Greek word commonly translated as "believe" ninety-eight separate times. Yet the Greek word for "faith" did not occur anywhere in the entire book. On the contrary, the concept of *trusting in God* as an active, doable, near-tangible endeavor seemed to be far more important to John. In that sense John was a true son of Abraham, whose *trust in Him* God accepted as righteousness, but who also *acted* on that trust in dramatic, physical ways.

This matches very closely with John's own example, and the examples of the other disciples as well. They had to move well beyond simple faith, all the way to *total trust* before they could give up everything else to follow Jesus Christ. They did so day after day, with no guarantee of any reward whatsoever beyond His promise of eternal life—and no examples to lean on except their own experience of Who and What Jesus Christ was.

The Savior. Of all humanity. Who came to sacrifice Himself for them in a drama that only God could conceive, to fit a purpose and satisfy a judgment that only He could fully understand. To generate a reward that only man could accept.

How This Study Guide Is Organized

Like so many other portions of the Bible, the book of John could be approached in any number of ways, ranging from a topical study of its major subjects to a verse-by-verse examination focusing on its tiniest parts, one by one. Entire books could be (and have been) written—for example—on the first verses of chapter 15 (the vine and the vinedresser), or on the simple exhortation of Christ Himself: "If you love Me, keep My commandments" (John 14:15 NKJV).

However, as with other study guides in this series, we have chosen the *sequential* method, meaning that we will examine the text in front-to-back order, but not necessarily chapter-by-chapter.

Indeed, the first chapter of this guide concentrates on the first eighteen verses of John, a section commonly thought of as an almost-formal *prologue*. As you might then expect, it is matched by an *epilogue* at the end of the book (chapter 21), suggesting once again that John had a clear sense of how he wanted to present his story, with both an identifiable introduction and a definite ending.

Finally, whether the book of John will become (or already is!) your favorite Gospel is not important in any larger sense. But it would certainly be understandable.

The 35 Miracles of Jesus Christ, as Reported in the Four Gospels

		Matt.	Mark	Luke	John
1	Turning water into wine, at Cana				2:1–11
2	Healing an official's son, at Capernaum				4:46–54
3	Delivering a demoniac in the synagogue, at Capernaum		1:21–28	4:33–37	
4	Healing Peter's wife's mother, at Capernaum	8:14–15	1:29–31	4:38–39	
5	First miraculous catch of fish, at the Sea of Galilee			5:1–11	
6	Cleansing a leper, in Galilee	8:2–4	1:40–45	5:12–15	
7	Healing a paralytic, at Capernaum	9:1–8	2:1–12	5:17–26	
8	Healing an infirm man at the Pool of Bethesda, in Jerusalem				5:1-15
9	Healing a man's withered hand, in Galilee	12:9–13	3:1–5	6:6–11	
10	Healing a centurion's servant, at Capernaum	8:5–13		7:1–10	
11	Raising a widow's son, at Nain			7:11–17	
12	Casting out a blind and dumb spirit, in Galilee	12:22–32		11:14–23	
13	Stilling a storm, on the Sea of Galilee	8:18–27	4:35–41	8:22–25	
14	Delivering a demoniac of Gadara, at Gadara	8:28–34	5:1–20	8:26–39	
15	Healing a woman with a hemorrhage, at Capernaum	9:20–22	5:25–34	8:43–48	
16	Raising Jairus's daughter, at Capernaum	9:18–26	5:22–43	8:41–56	
17	Healing two blind men, at Capernaum	9:27–31			
18	Casting out a dumb spirit, at Capernaum	9:32–34			
19	Feeding the 5,000, near Bethsaida	14:13–21	6:32–44	9:10–17	6:1–14
20	Walking on the water, on the Sea of Galilee	14:22–33	6:45–52		6:15–21
21	Casting a demon from a Syrophoenician's daughter, at Phoenicia	15:21–28	7:24–30		
22	Healing a deaf person with a speech impediment, at Decapolis		7:31–37		
23	Feeding the 4,000, at Decapolis	15:32–38	8:1–9		
24	Healing a blind man of Bethsaida, at Bethsaida		8:22–26		
25	Casting out a demon from a lunatic boy, on Mount Hermon	17:14–21	9:14–29	9:37–42	
26	Finding money in a fish's mouth, at Capernaum	17:24–27			
27	Healing a man born blind, in Jerusalem				9:1–7
28	Healing a woman infirm for 18 years, probably at Perea			13:10–17	
29	Healing a man with dropsy, at Perea			14:1–6	
30	Raising Lazarus, at Bethany				11:1–44
31	Cleansing 10 lepers, in Samaria			17:11–19	
32	Healing blind Bartimaeus, at Jericho	20:29–34	10:46–52	18:35–43	
33	Cursing a fig tree, in Jerusalem	21:18–19	11:12–14		
34	Healing Malchus's ear, in the Garden of Gethsemane in Jerusalem			22:49–51	
35	Second miraculous catch of fish, on the Sea of Galilee				21:1–13
	Totals	**20**	**18**	**20**	**8**

1 Prologue

John 1:1–18

Before We Begin . . .

What do you believe to be the relationship of Jesus Christ, the Son of God, to God the Father? Do they coexist? Are they separate entities, or one divine Being?

The book of John begins with a truly unique introduction—or *prologue.* It is not at all unusual for a Gospel to establish a historical setting, but in his first eighteen verses John creates what might be called a *theological* setting instead. It's as though he wants to be sure that we understand, before we even begin, both *who this "Jesus" is* and *where He came from.* Fill in the blanks for the very first verse, and then answer the questions that follow.

In the beginning was the Word*, and the* word *was with God, and the* Word *was God. (John 1:1 NKJV)*

What is your understanding of "Word" as it is used in this verse?

Jesus

What "beginning" do you believe John was talking about?

before the world began

How can a "Word" be "with" anyone?

The Greek word from which we get "Word" is *logos,* which means "that which is spoken; a speech; a statement." *How does this affect your understanding of this usage of the term "Word" in this context?*

Now fill in the blanks in the next four verses.

> *He was in the* beginning *with God. All* things *were made through Him, and without* Him *nothing was made that was made. In Him was life, and the* light *was the light of men. And the light shines in the darkness, and the darkness did not comprehend it. (John 1:2–5 NKJV)*

What "beginning" do you believe John is talking about here?

What did he mean by "things" that "were made"?

In what sense do you believe he meant that "the life was the light of men"?

What about "the darkness did not comprehend it"? In what sense can darkness comprehend—*or* fail to comprehend—*light?* the world "non-christians"

JOHN THE BAPTIST, WITNESS TO THE TRUE LIGHT

The next four verses describe a man named John—but not the same "John" who is writing the book! This John is more commonly known as *John the Baptist,* who (as we are told in the other Gospels, and in the book of Isaiah as well) came to prepare the way for Christ Himself. Fill in the blanks for the following verses, and then answer the questions below.

> *There was a man sent from God, whose name was* John*. This man came for a* [illegible]*, to bear witness of the Light, that all through him might* believe*. He was not that Light, but was sent to bear witness of that Light. That was the* true *Light which gives light to every man coming into the world. (John 1:6–9 NKJV)*

What does John mean by the word "witness" in verse 6? Witness to what? of God,

Notice the distinction between the words "Light" (with a capital L*) and "light" with a lowercase* l. *Why does John make this distinction? What is his purpose in doing so?*

Based on what John says here, who was greater—John the Baptist or the One John refers to as "the Light"?

The next four verses further describe Jesus Christ Himself, even though the author, John, has not yet called Him by the name by which most people know Him. Again, fill in the blanks in the text below, then answer the questions that follow.

> *He was in the __________, and the __________ was made through Him, and the __________ did not know Him. He came to His own, and His own did not receive Him. But as many as received Him, to them He gave the right to become children of God, to those who believe in His name: who were born, not of blood, nor of the will of the flesh, nor of the will of man, but of God. (John 1:10–13 NKJV)*

The word "world" is used three times in the first sentence above. In each case it is used in a slightly different sense. In the spaces provided, can you identify the "three senses" in which the word "world" is used?

1. He was in the world.

2. The world was made through Him.

3. The world did not know Him.

What's in a Name?

In recent years, much has been made of the "true" names of the man known to most of the world as *Jesus Christ,* His mother, *Mary,* and His brother *James.*

To clarify, the original Hebrew name of the Son of God, by which His earthly parents knew Him, is variously transliterated into English as *Yeshua, Yahshua,* or other variations. It was similar to the name of Moses' lieutenant, which is usually transliterated as *Joshua,* but it was not quite identical. In the original Hebrew it meant "I am salvation."

The difficulty in getting an absolutely *correct* transliteration, of course, is that the pictographic letters of the Hebrew language have no precise equivalents in English; only "soundalikes."

To complicate things further, His name came into English via Greek *(Iesous)* and Latin *(Jesu),* and thus became *Jesus* in English. Meanwhile, the word "Christ" derives from the Greek word *Christos,* meaning "anointed one."

Less familiar to many Christians is the correct Hebrew name of the mother of Christ, and that of his brother. His mother, *Miryam,* was given the English name *Mary* even though Moses' sister—who had exactly the same Hebrew name—was perhaps more accurately called *Miriam* in most English translations. Likewise, Christ's brother, *Ya'akov,* was given the English name *James* even though the combination of Hebrew-into-English letters that formed his name was transliterated as *Jacob* elsewhere in the Bible.

What did John mean by "He came to His own"? Who were "His own"?

What concept was John referring to in the last sentence of the passage above? What "right" did Christ give to those willing to do . . . what? What two things did John say we must do to receive this "right"?

THE WORD BECOMES FLESH

In typical Hebraic fashion, John does not write his book in a straight-ahead, linear fashion, with each thought following the preceding thought and with similar thoughts grouped together into what we know as "paragraphs." Next, he returns to the concept of "the Word" and begins to amplify his very first thoughts:

> *And the Word became flesh and dwelt among us, and we beheld His glory, the glory as of the only begotten of the Father, full of grace and truth. (John 1:14 NKJV)*

Then John returns to his introduction of John the Baptist, adding more details to what he told us earlier:

> *John bore witness of Him and cried out, saying, "This was He of whom I said, 'He who comes after me is preferred before me, for He was before me.' " (John 1:15 NKJV)*

Finally, John brought the prologue to a close with these words:

> *And of His fullness we have all received, and grace for grace. For the law was given through Moses, but grace and truth came through Jesus Christ. No one has seen God at any time. The only begotten Son, who is in the bosom of the Father, He has declared Him. (John 1:16–18 NKJV)*

What did John (the author) mean when he said that "the Word became flesh and dwelt among us" (v. 14)?

What did he say that "the only begotten of the Father" was filled with (v. 14)?

Why did John the Baptist claim that Jesus Christ was "preferred before me" (v. 15)?

What was given through Moses (v. 17)?

What came through Jesus Christ (v. 17)?

How do you believe these two elements complement each other?

WAS JESUS TRULY GOD IN THE FLESH?

The first verse of the book of John is generally considered the strongest evidence in the New Testament of the fundamental Christian belief that Jesus was and is *truly God.* Various people have argued, through the years, that the text should say "the Word was *a* god." However, according to a huge preponderance of Greek scholars who have studied this passage for centuries, nothing in the Greek text of this verse supports that argument. To translate it in any way other than the "standard" translation we have used here, which is already familiar to millions of believers around the world, would be (among other things) to suggest a form of polytheism. If Jesus is *"a"* God, He is not *"the"* God who created the universe.

At this point, take a few minutes to reread the Prologue (vv. 1–18) and look for the words in the first column of the following table. In column two, indicate in which verses each word occurs. Add up all the occurrences of each one in column three. Finally, in column four, under "meaning," indicate what you believe each of these words represents in the portion of John you've read so far.

From the Prologue to the Book of John

Word	Verses	Total	Meaning
light		6	
darkness		2	
witness		1	
true		1	
world		4	
Son	14, 18	2	
Father		2	
glory		2	
truth		2	
Word		4	
grace		3	

Congratulations! You have just created a matrix, featuring some of the most important theological concepts and constructs of the book of John, and indicating where they were first introduced by him within the first eighteen verses of his book. Keep this chart handy, for these words (and, more important, the concepts they represent) will occur many more times in the remaining chapters and verses of John.

It could be especially interesting to consider how your understanding of each of these words might change as you study the book of John in its entirety.

Pulling It All Together . . .

- John's prologue made it clear that *Word/Son/Jesus Christ* are all names for the same "person," who is totally one God, yet separate from God the Father. This concept is commonly known as the concept of the Trinity—one God, coexisting in three equal parts that are distinct from one another, yet the same. This is not an easy concept to grasp—indeed, it is one of the divine mysteries that simply cannot be fully explained in human terms.

- John the Baptist was sent ahead of Christ, to "bear witness to the Light." He is not to be confused with Christ Himself. Through the other Gospels we know that John the Baptist was actually Christ's cousin, but John himself did not tell us so.

- Theologically, the "salvation" we are offered through belief in Christ was and is identical to the salvation God offered through "belief in Himself" prior to Christ's coming. However, through His death on the cross (about which John will have much to say in later chapters, as do the other Gospels), Christ made it unnecessary for us to offer blood sacrifices to atone for our sins, as God's justice had required prior to Christ's sacrificial death. This is the "grace" God extended to us through the death of His Son—not the "grace" to sin as we wish, but the "grace" to be considered *righteous* in God's eyes via the atoning blood of Christ.

2 Early Ministry

John 1:19–7:9

Before We Begin . . .

What is your understanding of the relationship between Jesus Christ and John the Baptist? What did John the Baptist himself say about this relationship?

John Chapter 1, Continued . . .

Jesus and John the Baptist

The first portion of this section brings us back to John the Baptist and repeats certain conversations between him and "the Jews." The term "Jews," as used here, refers to the religious leaders of the city of Jerusalem, who are eventually identified as Pharisees (v. 24). Please read John 1:19–28 and answer the following questions.

What two groups of people did the Jews send to talk to John the Baptist?

What would be the differences between these two groups?

What did John the Baptist "confess"?

What do you think is meant by the word "confessed" in this context?

Why would they have asked John if he was Elijah?

they expected Elijah to announce the coming of christ

The next several verses (John 1:29–34) cover what some commentators call John's "second witness," in which he testified about who Jesus was.

In verse 29, why do you believe John called Jesus the "Lamb of God"? How would John be able to "make this connection" in his own mind?

Sacrafice for sins

What did he mean when he said that Jesus "was before me"? In what way?

Jesus was in the begining

Please fill in the blanks in the following verses.

> *And John bore witness, saying, "I saw the __________ descending from heaven like a __________, and He remained upon Him. I did not know Him, but He who sent me to __________ with water said to me, 'Upon whom you see the Spirit __________, and remaining on Him, this is He who baptizes with the Holy Spirit.' And I have seen and __________ that this is the Son of God." (John 1:32–34 NKJV)*

Of what two things did John the Baptist testify, concerning himself and Jesus?

1.

2.

Jesus Calls His Disciples

In the remainder of chapter 1, Jesus began to gather His disciples. Some of these verses can be tricky in terms of who was speaking and who was being spoken about. Sometimes it helps to follow the capitalization of the pronouns. For example, in verse 37, the "two disciples" were disciples of John the Baptist, whom they heard speak of Christ; they then followed Him (i.e., Christ). In a sense they *switched* from one teacher to another, which is undoubtedly what John the Baptist intended, for John (the writer) took great pains to clarify John the Baptist's divinely decreed role as one who "prepared the way" for Christ Himself.

The first words John recorded from the mouth of Jesus occur in verse 38 when He asked the same two disciples (whose names we do not yet know), "What do you seek?" This particular question was certainly simple on the surface, but could have had far larger implications. Likewise with their answer: "Rabbi, where are You staying?"

Read the remainder of this chapter (John 1:39–51) and answer the questions below.

According to this passage, who was the very first disciple whose name we are actually given?

Andrew

Who was this man's brother, who became the second disciple?

Peter

Who was their father? And, to what did Jesus change the second disciple's name?

?

Rock - what he would become

(Please note that, in verse 44, *Simon Peter [Cephas]* is now simply called *Peter*, which is how he was known throughout most of the New Testament.)

What did Philip say to Nathanael about Jesus?

We have found the one Moses & the prophets had written about

Locations of Some of the Miracles of Jesus Christ

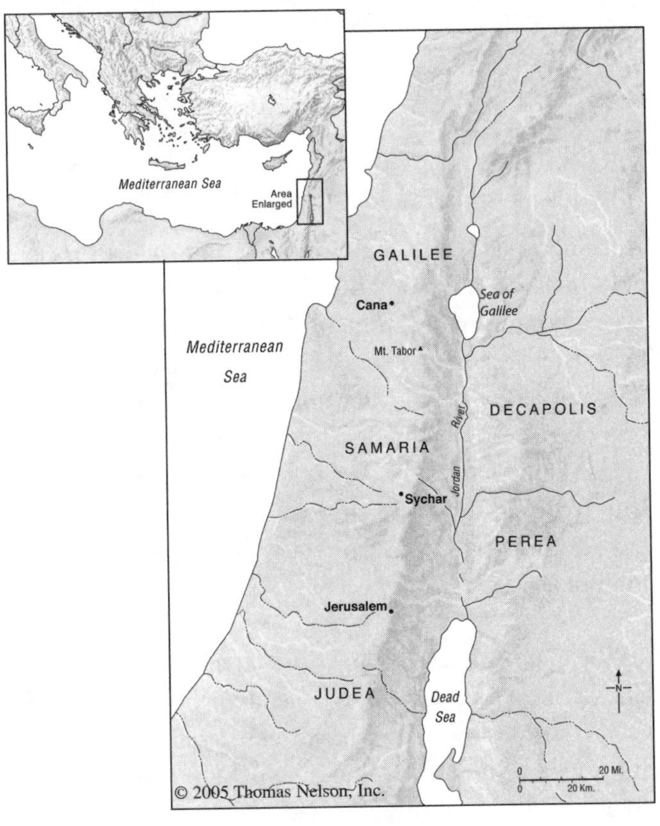

What was Nathanael's response?

Can anything good come from Nazareth

Why do you suppose Nathanael said that?

What was the first thing Jesus said, in turn, about Nathanael?

a true Israelite who there is nothing false

John Chapter 2

Miracle #1— Jesus Turns Water into Wine

Since not one of the four Gospels is an exhaustive, definitive, day-by-day history of Jesus' life on Earth, we cannot know precisely how many miracles He performed while He lived here. However, if you catalog all those that were recorded in the four Gospels, you will get a grand total of thirty-five *separate* ones. Many of these, of course, are repeated more than once—some in two different Gospels, some in three, and one (the feeding of the five thousand) in all four. Matthew and Luke both record twenty miracles, Mark records eighteen, and John records eight.

Of the eight miracles John included, he was the *only* chronicler of six. Obviously, he was extremely selective. Since his Gospel was also written last, his choices also suggest that—to at least some limited extent—he might have been filling in the record of the other three Gospels. Seven of the eight miracles he mentioned occurred during Jesus' life on Earth; the last one (the second miraculous catch of fish) occurred after His death and before He ascended into heaven—and this is also one of the six that John alone recorded.

The miracle mentioned in the beginning of chapter 2 is the first one that John recorded. Read John 2:1–12 and answer the following questions.

What was happening in Cana on this day?

Why do you suppose Jesus did not seem to want to perform this miracle?

"Wasnt his time"

What was unique about the wine Jesus created, with respect to the usual serving practice of that era?

It was best

JESUS CLEANSES THE TEMPLE

John's Gospel is the only one that records a cleansing of the temple at the beginning of Jesus' ministry; the others record the one that occurred just prior to His crucifixion. Most commentators believe there probably were two separate incidents, for some of the details are different. Read John 2:13–25 and answer the following questions.

For what reason did Jesus go to Jerusalem, in this story?

Passover

Why would people be selling oxen, sheep, and doves—and changing money—in the temple?

to use for offerings

What did He mean when He said, "Destroy this temple, and in three days I will raise it up"? What did His listeners think He meant?

JOHN CHAPTER 3

YOU MUST BE BORN AGAIN

The story of Nicodemus is told in the first twenty-one verses of chapter 3. Perhaps the most familiar verses are contained in the following passage, especially the verse in italics. Fill in the blanks as you read.

> *"Are you the teacher of ______, and do not know these things? Most assuredly, I say to you, We speak what We know and ______ what We have seen, and you do not receive Our ______. If I have told you earthly things and you do not believe, how will you ______ if I tell you ______ things? No one has ascended to heaven but He who came down from heaven, that is, the Son of Man who is in heaven. And as Moses lifted up the serpent in the wilderness, even so must the Son of Man be lifted up, that whoever believes in Him should not perish but have eternal life.* For God so loved the world that He gave His only begotten Son, that whoever believes in Him should not perish but have everlasting life. For God did not send His Son into the world to condemn the world, but that the world through Him might be saved."

"He who believes in Him is not ________, but he who does not believe is condemned already, because he has not ________ in the name of the only begotten Son of God. And this is the ________, that the light has come into the world, and men loved ________ rather than light, because their deeds were evil. For everyone practicing evil hates the light and does not come to the light, lest his deeds should be exposed. But he who does the ________ comes to the light, that his deeds may be clearly seen, that they have been done in God." (John 3:10–21 NKJV, emphasis added)

What Was Nicodemus Missing?

The story of Nicodemus has been told and retold countless times, but seldom has one of its more "interesting twists" been examined. When Jesus spoke of being born again in the spiritual sense, Nicodemus asked Him, "How can these things be?"

In response Jesus said: "Are you the teacher of Israel, and do not know these things?" This would seem to indicate that Nicodemus should have known what Jesus was speaking of—that being "born of the spirit" meant having one's faith in God accepted as righteousness by God, as exemplified by Abraham and taught by Moses. In other words, this should not have been a new doctrine to a "teacher of Israel." Perhaps the exact wording Jesus was using was somewhat different from what Nicodemus had heard before, but the concept should have been very familiar.

John the Baptist Exalts Christ

The final verses of chapter 3 contain another familiar quotation from John the Baptist, who was baptizing converts not far from where Jesus and His disciples came in the land of Judea. John's comment in verse 24, to the effect that John the Baptist "had not yet been thrown into prison," seems to suggest that John's own book was partly intended to supplement the other three Gospels, all of which mention John the Baptist's imprisonment by Herod, which eventually ended in his beheading.

Most revealing of John the Baptist's character is this quote in response to a question from one of his own disciples, who seemed to be lamenting Jesus' "intrusion" and John the Baptist's waning influence that came as a result:

> *John answered and said, "A man can receive nothing unless it has been given to him from heaven. You yourselves bear me witness, that I said, 'I am not the Christ,' but, 'I have been sent before Him.' He who has the bride is the bridegroom; but the friend of the bridegroom, who stands and hears him, rejoices greatly because of the bridegroom's voice. Therefore this joy of mine is fulfilled.* He must increase, but I must decrease. *He who comes from above is above all; he who is of the earth is earthly and speaks of the earth. He who comes from heaven is above all. (John 3:27–31 NKJV, emphasis added)*

John Chapter 4

A Samaritan Woman Meets Her Messiah

This chapter begins with the story of the Samaritan woman whom Jesus met at a well on the edge of a city called Sychar, in Samaria. John undoubtedly included this (along with the story of Nicodemus) to demonstrate that Christ could read the hearts of those He met. Read John 4:7–26 and answer the following questions.

Baptism vs. Mikveh

The Greek word for what John the Baptist did in the river Jordan, was *baptizo,* whence comes our word *baptize.* To the people of his own day, however, John the Baptist was known as *Yochanon the Immerser.*

More to the point, the ancient Hebrew cleansing ritual on which modern baptism is based was somewhat different in ancient days. First, it was always done, if possible, in running water. Second, the participant always faced directly toward the source of the water, symbolically facing God as the Source of life. Third, he or she knelt down and bowed *forward, toward* God in a symbolic sense, going completely under the water and thus "washing away" all impurities.

Fourth, though men like John the Baptist were available to assist (and might have been especially important in a river with a strong current), this was not his primary function. In ancient times, wherever possible the "*mikveh*" or "baptism" itself was completed without actual physical assistance, for it was understood to be entirely between God and the participants themselves. Thus, John called people to repentance and *assisted* in their baptism, but whether he himself actually " physically baptized" them (that is, whether he actually pushed them under the water and pulled them back up) introduces a fascinating semantic (and perhaps even a doctrinal) question that is well beyond the scope of this study guide . . . but worth looking into in the light of Old Testament understanding of the whole *mikveh*/baptism concept.

The woman of Samaria was not a Jew, but a Samaritan. How, then, did she know of Jesus and the "greatness" that He represented to the Jews? because of their conversation? She knew of the messiah & he said that was him

Where were Jesus' disciples while He talked to the woman?

in town getting food

What kind of water did Jesus say that He could give her?

eternal life

WAS JESUS A PHARISEE?

We know for certain that Paul was a trained rabbi and a Pharisee; he said so himself. Even though Christ had some harsh words of criticism for the Pharisees, most scholars also believe that He was a Pharisee as well, not least because many of His teachings paralleled (word-for-word, in some cases) those of well-known Pharisee scholars of history, such as Hillel and Gamliel (also spelled *Gamaliel*). The latter, in fact, was Paul's own teacher.

However, John the Baptist also provides a clue that is often overlooked. Note what John said when the Pharisees came from Jerusalem to question him about his own credentials:

> John answered them, saying, "I baptize with water, but there stands *One among you whom you do not know.* It is He who, coming after me, is preferred before me, whose sandal strap I am not worthy to loose." (John 1:26–27 NKJV, italics added)

At that point, did the woman understand what Jesus was saying?

no

What did He tell her would happen to all who drank of the water in her well? they will be thirsty again

What was the difference between that and the water He would give her? this they will never be thirsty & gives eternal life

When He told her to go and call her husband, what did she say?

I have no husband

Did she speak the truth? yes

How many husbands did Jesus say that she had had? And, was she married at the moment? 5 + no

Even though she was not a Jew, did the woman seem to have an understanding of the coming of Messiah? yes

Who did Jesus tell her that He was?

Miracle #2—Jesus Heals a Nobleman's Son

Near the end of chapter 4 we come to John's "second sign" (John 4:54), in which Jesus healed the dying son of a nobleman who pressed him for help. When Jesus told him to "go your way; your son lives," the man went home, to discover that his son got better at the precise moment when Christ spoke the words. (This miracle also occurred in Cana.)

John Chapter 5

Miracle #3—Jesus Heals a Man at the Bethesda Pool

This story contains the well-known "Take up your bed and walk" quotation, directed to the infirm man whom Jesus had just healed. Read John 5:1–15 and answer the questions below.

How many "porches" did the pool in Jerusalem called Bethesda have?

What was the superstition involving the pool, an angel, and the first one into the water? How do you suppose such a story got started?

How long had the infirm man in this story been sick?

Did Jesus put the man in the water, or did He heal him on His own? Why is that distinction significant?

The remainder of chapter 5 is an extended discourse on several key points, among them the following:

1. That all who honor God the Father should likewise honor the Son of God—and He was that Son.

2. That life and judgment both come through the Son of God, for God the Father has "committed all judgment to the Son" (John 5:22 NKJV) so that "all should honor the Son just as they honor the Father." (John 5:23 NKJV)

3. That Jesus, at this time, would not testify in His own behalf, but that John the Baptist had already testified brilliantly about Him—enough so that those who'd heard him should have been convinced.

4. That God the Father and the written Word had both testified in His behalf.

5. That His own deeds testified to His divinity, even though He wasn't asking them to accept His own word as a witness.

This section ends with the following passage.

> *"I do not receive honor from men. But I know you, that you do not have the love of God in you. I have come in My Father's name, and you do not receive Me; if another comes in his own name, him you will receive. How can you believe, who receive honor from one another, and do not seek the honor that comes from the only God? Do not think that I shall accuse you to the Father; there is one who accuses you—Moses, in whom you trust. For if you believed Moses, you would believe Me;*

for he wrote about Me. But if you do not believe his writings, how will you believe My words?" (John 5:41–47 NKJV)

JOHN CHAPTER 6

MIRACLE #4—JESUS FEEDS FIVE THOUSAND PEOPLE

The opening section of chapter 6 tells the familiar story of the feeding of the five thousand. Read John 6:1–15 and answer the following questions.

What "Sea" did Christ travel across before He fed the multitude?

Sea of Tiberias (Sea of Galilee

Why do you believe He then went "up on the mountain"? Why not just stay on the shore?

time to disciples

What did Philip basically tell Jesus about the bread situation?

8 months wages wouldn't be enough to feed all of them

How many loaves and fishes did Jesus use to feed the five thousand? 5 2

What did those who saw what Jesus had done say about Him as a result? Surely he is a prophet

WAS THERE A SHORTAGE OF BREAD?

In the introduction to the story of the feeding of the five thousand, we find these verses:

> Now the Passover, a feast of the Jews, was near. Then Jesus lifted up His eyes, and seeing a great multitude coming toward Him, He said to Philip, "Where shall we buy bread, that these may eat?" (John 6:4–5 NKJV)

One of the basic elements of the Passover observance was the removal of all *leavening* from the households of devout Jews. In Exodus 12:15, God commanded that this should be done on the first day of Passover, which He then identified as the fourteenth day of the first month, in Leviticus 23:5. But many Jews interpreted "on" to mean "by" and therefore removed all the leaven (i.e., yeast) from their houses *in the days leading up to Passover itself,* which would certainly not contradict the commandment and might be a savvy way to "play it safe."

So, given this dynamic, if "the Passover, a feast of the Jews, was near," when we read this story without thinking about the leavening issue, it's possible that we're missing one of the interesting dynamics of the overall scenario. Is it possible Jesus knew that obtaining enough "regular" leavened bread for five thousand people might be even more difficult than usual at that particular time?

MIRACLE #5—JESUS WALKS ON THE SEA

Next, John told the story of the fifth miracle he deemed significant enough to include in his Gospel. Fill in the blanks in the passage below.

> *Now when evening came, His ____________ went down to the sea, got into the boat, and went over the sea toward ____________. And it was already dark, and Jesus had not come to them. Then the ____________ arose because a great wind was blowing. So when they had rowed about three or four miles, they saw Jesus ____________ on the sea and drawing near the boat; and they were afraid. But He said to them, "It is I; do not be*

afraid.” Then they willingly received Him into the boat, and immediately the boat was at the shore where they were going. (John 6:16–21 NKJV)

MORE TEACHINGS FROM JESUS

Read the remainder of chapter 6 and the beginning of chapter 7 (John 6:22–7:9), and answer the following questions.

What does Jesus indicate is “the work of God” in verse 29?

to believe in Jesus

What does Jesus say is the will of “Him who sent Me” in verse 40?

Everyone who believes in Jesus will have eternal life

In verse 47, what did Jesus say that “he who believes in Me” has?

everlasting life

What did He call Himself in verse 48?

bread of life

What did Simon Peter tell Jesus the disciples had "come to believe" in verse 69? that Jesus is the Messiah

Who was the "devil" Jesus spoke of in verses 70–71?

Judas

What did Jesus mean, in John 7:8, when He said, "My time has not yet fully come"? He still had work to do & it wasn't time for his persecution & death

Pulling It All Together . . .

- John "recorded" Jesus' baptism by John the Baptist, but concentrated on their conversation rather than the details of the actual event.

- John recorded eight separate miracles of Jesus, seven during His life on Earth "in the flesh" and one more after His resurrection but before His ascension into heaven. The section of the book of John covered in this chapter includes the first five.

- The feeding of the five thousand, surely one of the best-known miracles of Jesus, is also the only one recorded in all four Gospels.

3 LATER MINISTRY

JOHN 7:10–12:50

Before We Begin . . .

When you think of the story of Lazarus, what first comes to mind? Why do you think it was such a big event?

JOHN CHAPTER 7

In the first few verses of chapter 7 (which were covered in chapter 2 of this guide), Jesus explained to His disciples that He would not be "going up" to Jerusalem with them for the Feast of Tabernacles. His reasons were simple—He knew that certain people were already plotting against His life, but His time had not yet come. So He went in secret—although He did not remain incognito for long!

GOING UP?

Unlike the modern expression often used in elevators, this Hebrew travel idiom, used several times in the Gospels with reference to the journey to Jerusalem, could have had both geographical and theological implications. Jerusalem was in the hills, so going there from the surrounding land required the traveler to "go up" in a geographic (or physical) sense. Also, *going up* could refer to a theological or spiritual journey—certainly, when Jesus returned to Jerusalem for His crucifixion later on He was *going up, or back,* to the Father.

What Is the Feast of Tabernacles?

The Feast of Tabernacles, also called *Succoth,* was ordained by God in Leviticus 23:33–36. It was a happy time of thanksgiving for the harvest just completed; it was also intended to remind the Jews of how God had "tabernacled" with them in the desert when they first came out of Egypt. For this reason, many devout Jews of that day (and down to the present) gathered together and lived for several days in booths made out of branches and other natural materials. Nowadays, of course, it is possible to buy a complete prefabricated "Succoth booth" and erect it outdoors at the appropriate time.

The Heavenly Scholar

Read John 7:10–31, and answer the following questions.

Based on your understanding of what we have indicated thus far (and of your own reading), who were "the Jews" of verses 11 and 13? Does this term refer to the common people or to some of the leaders?

What was the general feeling about Jesus among the common people?

In verse 14, where did Jesus go to teach? Why would He go there?

Who did Jesus claim was the source of what He taught?

What was one measure of righteousness by which Jesus told the people they should judge Him, in verses 16–18?

What was the reference to Moses, in verse 19, all about? How did Jesus then extend this comparison to teach a broader truth, in verses 21–24?

What did "some of them from Jerusalem" admit in verse 25—not about themselves but about "they"?

What was part of the confusion surrounding Jesus' origin (v. 27)? What mistake did people tend to make? (Hint: Refer back to Nathanael's very first comment when he met Jesus in John 1:46!)

Jesus and the Religious Leaders

It didn't take long for Jesus' own words to begin working against Him. Soon the leaders of the Pharisees heard the crowd murmuring and sent officers to take Him prisoner. To see how Jesus responded, fill in the blanks in the following passage:

> *On the last day, that great day of the feast, Jesus stood and cried out, saying, "If anyone __________, let him come to Me and drink. He who believes in Me, as the __________ has said, out of his heart will flow rivers of*

__________ water." But this He spoke concerning the Spirit, whom those believing in Him would receive; for the Holy Spirit was not yet given, because Jesus was not yet __________. (John 7:37–39 NKJV)

The authorities still did not recognize Jesus, even though some of the people reiterated two of the ancient prophecies concerning Him: that He would be of the lineage of David, and that He would come from Bethlehem. However, one man whom Jesus had already ministered to spoke on His behalf.

Who was this man, and what did he say of Jesus, in verses 50–51?

John Chapter 8

Jesus, the Light of the World

The entire eighth chapter of John is an extended dialogue between Jesus and the religious leaders in Jerusalem—the scribes and the Pharisees. It began when He went into the temple to teach, at which point they brought to Him a woman "caught in adultery" and challenged Him to condemn her to death.

Read John 8:1–11 and answer the following questions.

What did Jesus do while the leaders were accusing the woman and challenging Jesus to condemn her?

Why, in verse 6, does the Bible say they did this?

What is the answer He eventually gave to them?

What happened next?

Based on all this, how would you describe Jesus' personal style? How did He deal with confrontations?

What was His final answer to the woman herself?

How do you, personally, feel about the way Jesus treated this woman?

Jesus Defends His Self-Witness

Next, Jesus was accused of being a false witness. Fill in the blanks in the passage below to see how He answered.

> *Jesus answered and said to them, "Even if I bear ______ of Myself, My witness is true, for I know where I came from and where I am going; but you do not know where I come from and where I am going. You ______ according to the flesh; I judge no one. And yet if I do judge, My ______ is true; for I am not alone, but I am with the ______ who sent Me. It is also written in your law that the testimony of two men is true. I am One who bears witness of Myself, and the Father who sent Me bears ______ of Me." (John 8:14–18 NKJV)*

How did Jesus use the law, in this passage, to point out their hypocrisy?

Read John 8:21–36 and answer the following questions.

Where does Jesus say the leaders are from? How does He contrast this with where He Himself came from?

In verse 24, what does Jesus say will be the consequence of their refusal to believe in Him?

death

In verse 28, what do you believe Jesus meant when He said, "When you lift up the Son of Man . . ."? What does "lift up" mean in this context?

the cross

The Truth Shall Make You Free

In verse 32, Jesus spoke the well-known phrase in the heading above. What did He mean by this remark, in a theological context? How can "truth" set anyone "free"?

free from sin

Did the people Jesus was speaking to, as shown in verse 33, understand what He was saying? If not, why?

More Difficult Questions

In the next several verses (John 8:37–59), Jesus makes a clear comparison between His accusers and the legitimate descendants of Abraham. Read these verses and answer the following "thought" questions.

What is the general principle Jesus was explaining in this passage? How does it relate to the concept of "ancestry"?

Who did Jesus say was the actual "father" of those He was speaking to?

In what sense did He mean this?

Does it seem to you that Jesus was being confrontational on purpose? If so, why would He do so?

What other principle did Jesus repeat here, once again? About honor?

Why do you suppose John chose to repeat so carefully these particular words of Jesus?

Here are three more "thought" questions, all linked together:

Do you believe that any "reasonable person," being confronted and taught by Jesus in this manner and this situation, would recognize Him for who He was? What would you have thought if you *were there?*

To what extent was He "doing the work of His Father" and purposely bringing about His own eventual fate?

Why would He do such a thing?

MIRACLE #6—HEALING A MAN WHO WAS BLIND FROM BIRTH

The entire ninth chapter of the book of John concerns a man who was blind from birth, whom Jesus healed. John's Gospel is the only one that records this specific story. Undoubtedly, John selected it for specific reasons, which could have included the following:

1. He wanted to show the clear divinity of Jesus, by demonstrating that Jesus was capable not only of curing a temporary illness but also of *healing a lifelong affliction.* Also, ancient Jewish tradition taught that only the true Messiah would be able to heal lifelong blindness.

2. He wanted to further demonstrate the resistance of the religious leaders toward the work Jesus was doing among the people.

3. He wanted to demonstrate that Jesus was not only *capable,* but that He could literally use *any method He chose* to accomplish His purposes.

JOHN CHAPTER 9

Please read the ninth chapter of John; then answer the questions below.

How do you suppose Jesus and His disciples knew that the blind man in this story had been blind from birth? Was it just "small-town syndrome" or something else?

Why would His disciples think someone had to have sinned to produce the man's blindness?

What did Jesus say was, instead, the reason for the man's blindness?

How do you imagine that a man who was blind from birth, suddenly given sight, would adjust to his brand-new vision?

In verse 16, what commandment did the Pharisees misuse to prove that Jesus (in their minds) was "not from God"?

Why Did Jesus Heal Someone Blind from Birth?

Jesus was obviously capable of performing any miracle He chose, but this particular one includes fascinating implications that might escape the casual reader.

Modern science tells us that a person who is born with normal sight will develop certain capabilities within their *sight mechanisms* that a person born blind will not develop. In a sense, it's comparable to what happens when a person loses their hearing. They can continue to talk, although they might gradually lose some of their ability to articulate because of their inability to hear what they are saying. In contrast, it is much more difficult for a person born deaf to learn to speak clearly, because they have no point of reference—no feel for what words "sound" and feel like within their lips, tongue, and teeth.

So it is with blindness. Thus, John recounted the one example in which Christ Himself chose to do the most difficult miracle. That is, not just to *restore* a person's *lost* sight but to give it to him for the first time, and to also do whatever was necessary, in a physical sense, to allow the man to use this gift instantly . . . that is, to know what he was suddenly seeing, and *what* it meant.

What was the logical response, by "others," within the same verse?

What did the formerly blind man say, in verse 17, about Jesus?

When the religious leaders brought in the blind man's parents, why did those parents insist that the leaders let the once-blind man speak for himself? What were they afraid of?

True Vision and True Blindness

After Jesus heard that the religious leaders had thrown the man out of the synagogue, He found him and identified Himself as the Son of God, at which point the man worshiped Him. The text then continues:

> *And Jesus said, "For judgment I have come into this world, that those who do not see may see, and that those who see may be made blind." Then some of the Pharisees who were with Him heard these words, and said to Him, "Are we blind also?" Jesus said to them, "If you were blind, you would have no sin; but now you say, 'We see.' Therefore your sin remains." (John 9:39–41 NKJV)*

What do you think Jesus meant in the last lines, beginning with "If you were blind, you would have no sin"?

John Chapter 10

Jesus the Good Shepherd

The tenth chapter of John is another familiar, extended parable in which Jesus compares Himself to a shepherd, calling Himself the Good Shepherd. Read the entire chapter and answer the following questions.

In verses 1–6, Jesus used an illustration involving sheep who know the voice of their own shepherd, which seems clear enough. But what did He mean when He extended the metaphor and spoke about sheep who do not follow a stranger, "for they do not know the voice of strangers" (v. 5)?

Could this also be interpreted as a warning, for all people, in all eras? In what sense?

Why do you think the people listening to Jesus, once again, did not understand Him?

Fill in the blanks in the following passage, which ends with an especially familiar verse.

> *"The thief does not come except to __________, and to __________, and to __________. I have come that they may have life, and that they may have it more abundantly. I am the __________ __________. The good shepherd gives His life for the sheep. But a hireling, he who is not the shepherd, one who does not own the sheep, sees the __________ coming and leaves the sheep and flees; and the wolf catches the sheep and scatters them. The hireling flees because he is a hireling and does not care about the sheep. I am the good shepherd; and I know My sheep, and am known by My own. As the __________ knows Me, even so I know the Father; and I lay down My life for the __________. And other sheep I have which are not of this fold; them also I must bring, and they will hear My voice; and there will be one flock and one shepherd. Therefore My Father loves Me, because __________ __________ __________ __________ __________ that I may take it again. No one takes it from Me, but I lay it down of Myself. I have power to lay it down, and I have power to take it again. This command I have received from My Father." (John 10:10–18 NKJV)*

What do verses 10–21 tell you about the reaction Jesus provoked from those who heard Him?

New Efforts to Stone Jesus

Verse 31 tells us that some of the Jews took up stones to stone Him. What was His response, in verse 32?

And what was their response to Him, in verse 33?

Two of the most powerful verses of this chapter, verses 37–38, are included here. Simply read them again and concentrate on appreciating the infallible logic of Christ!

> *"If I do not do the works of My Father, do not believe Me; but if I do, though you do not believe Me, believe the works, that you may know and believe that the Father is in Me, and I in Him." (John 10:37–38 NKJV)*

John, Chapter 11

Miracle #7—Jesus Raises Lazarus

Chapter 11 of John tells the story of Lazarus. As with other events, John's is the only Gospel to record this story, and it appears that he did so for a definite purpose—to demonstrate, once again, that Jesus Christ was the promised Messiah, capable of performing all the "benchmark" miracles of Jewish tradition and teachings. Note also, in verse 2, that John refers to the sister of Martha as "that Mary who anointed the Lord with fragrant oil," as told in Mark 14:3–9. John also mentions her elsewhere in his own Gospel, but not until chapter 12:1–10.

For now, read through the entire chapter and answer the following questions.

Where did Lazarus live before he died?

In verse 4, what did Jesus say Lazarus's sickness was "not unto"?

Why, then, does He say it happened?

In verse 16, Thomas (he of "doubting" fame as brought forth much later in the book of John) says, "Let us go also, that we may die with Him." What do you think he meant by this? Was this a statement of willingness to follow "unto death," or something else?

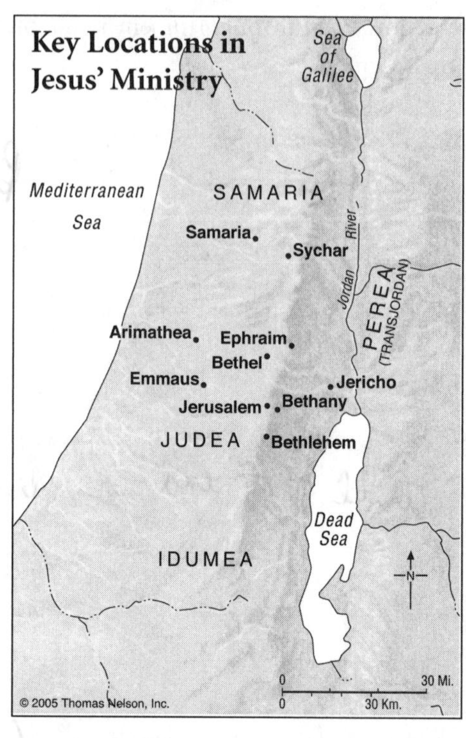

I Am the Resurrection and the Life

In verses 18–19 we are told that Bethany was only about two miles from Jerusalem, and that many people had joined Martha and Mary to comfort them. Would "many people" be a good thing from Jesus' perspective? If so, why?

What classic reference to Himself and His coming sacrifice for us did Jesus make in verses 25–26?

When Lazarus came forth he was "bound hand and foot with graveclothes" (v. 44). So, how do you believe he "came forth" on his own?

What did Jesus do just before He called Lazarus forth? What lesson might we find in this?

When John quoted Caiaphas in verses 49–50 (Caiaphas was the high priest that year), he then followed that with verse 51 in which he explained why Caiaphas spoke as he did. Why did John do this—was it necessary for our understanding, or was he embellishing an important point?

John Chapter 12

Once More to Jerusalem

This chapter concludes what we arbitrarily call the ending of the main phase of Jesus' ministry on earth. Once again it is almost time for the Feast of the Passover, and once again—like all other observant Jews of His time—Jesus went to Jerusalem to participate in the feast . . . or so it seems to those around Him. In reality, of course, Passover will be the day of His crucifixion. But first He had a few more people to talk to, and a few more teachings to bring forth.

Why Was the Raising of Lazarus So Important?

The ancient Jews believed that the soul of a dead person did not depart immediately—that it essentially "stayed with the body" for a period of up to three days after the person died. They were also warned in several places in the Old Testament about defiling themselves with dead bodies—they were literally not even to be in the room with a dead body, which was even more important for the Levites (the priests).

All four of the Gospels combined record just three examples of Jesus' raising someone from the dead. Of those three, only in the case of Lazarus is it made crystal clear that the deceased was dead for a full three days before Jesus raised him up. In contrast, the son of the woman of Nain (Luke 7:11–17) had almost assuredly not been dead three days, for when Jesus arrived he was just then being carried outside the city for burial. Likewise with the daughter of Jairus (Matt. 9:18–26; Mark 5:22–43; Luke 8:41–56), who died a very short time before Jesus arrived.

But Lazarus was a special case. Some scholars believe Jesus purposely let enough time pass so He could satisfy the ancient benchmark for the Jews' Messiah and raise someone who had been dead for three days or more (Lazarus had been dead four days—verse 17). Speaking of Lazarus's death, Jesus even said to His own disciples: "Lazarus is dead. And I am glad for your sakes that I was not there, that you may believe" (John 11:14–15 NKJV).

Notice, however, that He did not go inside the tomb but instead stood outside and called Lazarus to come forth on his own. Granted, it might seem strange to some people to claim that the pure Son of God Himself could be defiled by *anything*, but it is at least possible that Jesus was purposely honoring the prohibitions that applied to earthly priests. And remember, He *was* a *human being* even as He was God. Plus, God the Father cannot be in the presence of sin; note in Ezekiel 44:13 (NKJV) how the ancient priests who ministered to Him within the Most Holy Place would instantly die if they committed a sin—purposely or otherwise—in His presence.

In any case, whether the belief that the soul stayed with the body for three days was (or is) accurate is also not the point. Through the miracles He performed, Jesus sometimes seemed to be dealing with the ancient Jews' *perceptions* of reality, so they would have all the proof they should have needed, that He was who He said He was.

As before, read the entire twelfth chapter and then answer the questions below.

In the first few verses we are told that Jesus returned to Bethany on His way into Jerusalem, and ate supper with Lazarus, Martha, and Mary. What did Mary then do? poor expensive

perfume on his feet

What was the reaction of Judas Iscariot?

complained it could have been sold + given to the poor

Why was Judas's reaction especially hypocritical?

he, as the keeper of the money, would have taken some for himself

With what well-known quote did Jesus "cap off" His response to Judas's hypocrisy? Fill in the blanks below:

> *But Jesus said, "Let her alone; she has kept this for the day of My burial.* _you_ _will_ _always_ _have_ _the_ _poor_ _among_ _you_, *but* _you_ _will_ _not_ _always_ _have_ _me_*." (John 12:7–8 NKJV)*

Why did the chief priests plot against Lazarus?

because of his return from the dead, many were believing in Jesus

In verse 13, who is declared "blessed"?

is he who comes in the name of the Lord - Jesus

In verse 16, what does John say about Jesus' disciples, with respect to the prophecies Jesus fulfilled through His entrance into Jerusalem? they didn't understand until after his death, resurrection & assumption

Fill in the blanks for the following passage, one of Jesus' best-known teachings.

> *"The hour has come that the Son of Man should be* glorified*. Most assuredly, I say to you, unless a grain of wheat falls into the* ground *and* dies*, it remains alone; but if it dies, it* produces *much grain. He who* loves *his life will lose it, and he who hates his life in this world will keep it for* eternal *life. If anyone serves Me, let him follow Me; and where I am, there My* Father *will be also. If anyone* honors *Me, him My Father will honor." (John 12:23–26 NKJV)*

What did the people believe was "thunder" in verses 28–29?

God the Father

Verse 37 says that "although He had done so many signs before them, they did not believe in Him." Why did He do these signs?

to fulfill Isaiah's prophecy

Verse 42 tells us that certain rulers believed in Jesus. Why did they not confess it? Whose praise did they crave more than that of God? they prefer Man's praise to God

The last seven verses of chapter 12 contain another familiar message from Jesus. Who does He say those who believe in Him actually believe in (v. 44)? God the Father

Who did Jesus say those who see Him actually see?

God

Why do you believe Jesus was so careful to make it clear that He did only what God the Father directed Him to do?

PULLING IT ALL TOGETHER . . .

- Jesus performed miracles and taught miraculous things, but the religious authorities of His day would not recognize His deity.

- Jesus saved a woman from being stoned and did not "judge" her harshly, telling her to "go and sin no more" when her accusers had gone.

- Jesus claimed that the people who sought His death were not the legitimate descendants of Abraham, but of the devil . . . for their thoughts and deeds betrayed them.

- Jesus gave sight to a man who had been blind from birth. The same man believed in Jesus, but the authorities expelled him from the synagogue anyway.

- Jesus proclaimed Himself to be the Good Shepherd, the one true Light, and made other similar statements as well.

- Jesus resurrected Lazarus from the dead.

- Jesus wound up His earthly ministry by going to Jerusalem for Passover, where He knew that He would be "lifted up" and crucified.

4 PREPARING HIS DISCIPLES

JOHN 13:1–15:10

Before We Begin . . .

What is your understanding of the character of Judas Iscariot? Why do you think he did what he did?

By this point in his Gospel, John has presented all seven of the signs (or *miracles*) from Jesus' life, which he seemed to consider most important (see "Seven Signs of Jesus' Ministry" elsewhere in this chapter). He has also presented Jesus' triumphal entry into Jerusalem, although John's version does not give us as much detail (or sound as exuberant) as some of the other Gospels (for example, see Luke 19:28–48).

SEVEN SIGNS OF JESUS' MINISTRY

Sign or Miracle Indicating His Divinity	Possible Meaning
Turns water into wine (John 2:1–12)	Jesus is the Source of life/joy.
Heals a nobleman's son (John 4:46–54)	Jesus is Master over distance.
Heals a lame man at the pool of Bethesda (John 5:1–17)	Jesus is Master over time.
Feeds five thousand (John 6:1–14)	Jesus is the Bread of Life.
Walks on water; stills a storm (John 6:15–21)	Jesus is Master over nature.
Heals a man blind from birth (John 9:1–41)	Jesus is the Light of the World.
Raises Lazarus from the dead (John 11:17–45)	Jesus has power over death.

Now, with the Last Supper, John began the countdown to Jesus' death and resurrection. In the next three chapters, John concentrated on what were essentially Jesus' last words to His disciples, on subjects of obvious importance to Him, to them, and to us.

The Feasts of Passover and Firstfruits

The Hebrew word for Passover is *Pesach.* It means "to pass or jump over," which is what happened on the original Passover when the angel of death "jumped" or "passed over" all the doorposts to which the children of Israel had applied the blood of the first Passover lamb.

Both the Last Supper and Jesus' crucifixion happened on the same day (Passover) according to the Jewish calendar, for a day began at sundown and ended twenty-four hours later at the next sundown. In fact, many scholars believe that Jesus died on the cross at the same time (three o'clock in the afternoon) as the last Passover lamb for that year was slain by the high priest.

The Festival of Firstfruits occurred the first day following the Sabbath after Passover, which corresponded to the day of Jesus' resurrection. At Firstfruits, the very first of the harvest was offered to the Lord, just as Jesus was resurrected from the dead: "But now Christ is risen from the dead, and has become the firstfruits of those who have fallen asleep" (1 Cor. 15:20 NKJV).

John Chapter 13

Disciples Must Be Servants

Please read chapter 13 and answer the questions below.

How, according to verse 1, did Jesus feel about "His own" to the very end of His life?

What does verse 2 tell us had already been put into the heart of Judas Iscariot, even before the Feast of the Passover (i.e., the Last Supper) had ended?

What was the attitude Jesus was modeling in verses 6–8?

What is the obvious lesson in all this, for us today, as explained by Jesus in verses 12–17?

Who did Jesus say is not greater than his master?

JESUS IDENTIFIES HIS BETRAYER

What do you think the expression "lifted up his heel against Me" (v. 18) means?

What do you believe Jesus meant in verse 20 when He said, "He who receives Me receives Him who sent Me"?

Verse 23 provides an interesting reference to "one of His disciples, whom Jesus loved." Who was this disciple?

What did Jesus mean by "What you do, do quickly" in verse 27?

Extending a Piece of Bread

When the host of an ancient Hebrew meal handed someone a piece of bread, it was considered a powerful sign of friendship. The same might even be true today in our modern culture, in somewhat of a "general" way, but in that era, in that culture, it had a very definite, positive meaning. Indeed, throughout the Bible we are given examples of what might be called the "extraordinary significance" of breaking bread together, from the positive experience of Abraham and Melchizadek (Gen. 14:18) to the negative experience of David and his soldiers when David asked for help from Nabal (1 Sam. 25:4–38).

In such an overall context, the passage below has profound meaning:

> Jesus answered, "It is he to whom I shall give a piece of bread when I have dipped it." And having dipped the bread, He gave it to Judas Iscariot, the son of Simon. Now after the piece of bread, Satan entered him. Then Jesus said to him, "What you do, do quickly." (John 13:26–27 NKJV)

Some commentators believe that Jesus was literally extending to Judas Iscariot a last chance at genuine friendship—a final opportunity to avoid his sad eventual end. But as John tells us, even as Judas took the bread he made the contrary decision to betray his Master.

THE NEW COMMANDMENT

Fill in the blanks in the passage below.

> *So, when he had gone out, Jesus said, "Now the Son of Man is __________, and God is __________ in Him. If God is __________ in Him, God will also __________ Him in Himself, and __________ Him immediately. Little children, I shall be with you a little while longer. You will seek Me; and as I said to the Jews, 'Where I am going, you cannot come,' so now I say to you. A new __________ I give to you, that you __________ one another; as I have loved you, that you also love one another. By this all will know that you are My __________, if you have love for one another." (John 13:31–35 NKJV)*

In verse 38, what did Jesus predict that Peter would do, very early the next morning?

JOHN CHAPTER 14

THE WAY, THE TRUTH, AND THE LIFE

The next two chapters include some of Jesus' most familiar comments, spoken directly to His disciples but certainly applying to all others as well. Some of these are especially poignant; for example, John 14:2–3 can be seen as a reference to ancient Hebrew wedding customs wherein a young man, once betrothed to his beloved, then went home and spent his engagement period building a place (often an addition to his father's house) for his eventual bride to come and live with him.

Please read chapter 14 and answer the following questions.

Why did Jesus say our hearts should not be troubled? What should we do (note the active mode of this command) instead?

Fill in the words to the following verse.

> *Jesus said to him, "I am the __________, the __________, and the __________. No one __________ __________ __________ __________ except __________ Me." (John 14:6 NKJV)*

In verse 7, who did Jesus say we would also know if we knew Him?

In verse 9, who did He say we have also seen if we have seen Him?

Who did He say provided the authority for the words He spoke?

In your view, what is the great promise of verses 12–14?

In verse 16, Jesus spoke of giving us "another helper." What do you believe He was referring to?

In verse 18, "as what" did He promise He will not leave us?

What did Jesus say that "anyone who loves Me" will keep, in verse 23?

What will the Father do in return?

What did He say that anyone who does not *love Him will* not *do (v. 24)?*

What two things did Jesus promise that "the Helper" whom He identified here as "the Holy Spirit, whom the Father will send in My name," will do for the disciples—and hence for us (v. 26)?

1.

2.

What did He also promise to "leave with us" in verse 27?

In verse 30, who is the "ruler of this world" Jesus referred to? What did He mean when He said that this ruler "has nothing in Me"?

John Chapter 15

The True Vine

The first ten verses of this chapter are surely among the most familiar in the entire book of John. They have been used countless times to illustrate fundamental Christian concepts, including . . .

- Bearing fruit
- Being pruned by God
- Being grafted-in to Israel
- Fully abiding in Christ
- Emulating Christ and keeping God's commandments

Please read John 15:1–10, then answer the following questions.

Who is the true vine?

Who is the vinedresser?

What does the vinedresser do to every branch that does not bear fruit?

What does He do even to those branches that do *bear fruit?*

Who are we told to "abide" in?

What happens to anyone who does not abide in Him?

What shall be done for those who abide in Him, with His words abiding in them (v. 7)?

If we keep His commandments, what will we abide in?

What is the relationship between Jesus and the Father, as explained in verse 10?

PULLING IT ALL TOGETHER . . .

- Christ's example at the Last Supper tells us very clearly that we are to be the servants of others.

- That we love one another as He has loved us, is a direct commandment from Christ Himself.

- The vine/vinedresser metaphor (or parable) of John 15 is one of the best-known, most-quoted sections of the book of John.

5 FURTHER PREPARATIONS

JOHN 15:11–17:26

Before We Begin . . .

In thinking about the Last Supper, what aspect seems most significant to you?

According to John, Jesus did quite a bit of teaching at the Last Supper. Do you remember the lessons He taught?

In this section, Jesus continued His discourse with His disciples at the Last Supper. As is true of so many portions of John's Gospel, this section also contains a number of well-known verses and familiar concepts, beginning with a repetition of His commandment to "love one another" and continuing with a discussion of the world's *automatic hatred* for the things and the people of God. Please read John 15:11–27 and answer the following questions.

JOHN CHAPTER 15, CONTINUED . . .

What did Christ say (v. 11) that He wants to "remain in you" (i.e., in all of His followers) as a result of His teachings?

What is the commandment in verse 12 that He repeated from a previous chapter?

What is His definition of the greatest love of all in verse 13?

What is the difference between one who is His friend and one who is His servant, as clarified by Jesus in verses 14–15?

Who chose whom with respect to Jesus and His disciples?

THE WORLD'S HATRED

Fill in the blanks for the following passages.

> *"If the world hates you, you know that it __________ Me before it __________ you. If you were of the world, the world would __________ its own. Yet because you are not of the world, but I chose you out of the world, therefore the world __________ you." (John 15:18–19 NKJV)*

> *"Remember the word that I said to you, 'A __________ is not greater than his master.' If they __________ Me, they will also __________ you. If they kept My __________, they will keep yours also. But all these*

things they will do to you for My __________ __________, because they do not know Him who sent Me." (John 15:20–21 NKJV)

What is the condition Jesus mentioned in verse 22 under which He said that "they would have no sin"? What did He then say they do not have "for" their sin?

Why did Jesus say, in verse 23, that anyone who hates Him hates His Father also?

What is the next condition, mentioned in verse 24, under which He also said "they would have no sin"?

What did Jesus say, in verse 25, was "written in their law"? (Note: Rather than "law," some scholars would prefer the word "Scriptures," as in what some believe are messianic references in, for example, Psalms 35:19 and 69:4, as well as other places.)

In verse 26, who did Jesus say will testify of Him when He comes? Whom do you believe this "person" will be?

JOHN CHAPTER 16

JESUS WARNS AND COMFORTS HIS DISCIPLES

In this chapter, Jesus continued His message of hope, comfort, and promise to His disciples. Read the entire chapter and answer the questions that follow.

Why did Jesus say He was speaking "these things" to His disciples, in verse 1?

What two things did He say will be done to them, in verse 2?

1.

2.

Why, in verse 3, did He say people will do these things to His disciples?

Why did He say He did not say these things to them "at the beginning" (v. 4)? Why do you believe He would say that?

KILLING IN THE NAME OF GOD

John 16:1–3 (NKJV) says:

> These things I have spoken to you, that you should not be made to stumble. They will put you out of the synagogues; yes, the time is coming that whoever kills you will think that he offers God service. And these things they will do to you because they have not known the Father nor Me.

Are there people in the world today who are taught that killing Christians is a service to God?

Why did He say that it would be to their advantage if He went away (v. 7)?

What three things will the Helper do when He comes, and why will He do these things, as explained in verses 8–11?

1. Convict the world of guilt

Because

2.

Because

3.

Because

What did He say the Spirit of Truth would guide them into, when He came?

On what authority will the Spirit of Truth speak (v. 13)? Whom will He glorify, in verse 14?

To whom did Jesus say that all things the Father has also belong, *in verse 15?*

THE PENTECOST/SHAVUOT CONNECTION

Most Christians are aware that Jesus' death and resurrection occurred on two of the seven Jewish festivals given to them by God in Leviticus 23. He died on Passover and arose on Firstfruits. But many are not aware of another significant Jewish festival on which the *third* major event connected to Jesus' death and resurrection occurred.

This was the sending of the Holy Spirit to abide within the hearts of believers, which Jesus promised to do during His final discourse with the disciples at the Last Supper. This occurred on the fiftieth day after the first day of Passover, when Jews from all over the ancient world were in Jerusalem. Modern believers know this day as *Pentecost,* after the Greek word for *fifty.* But *Pentecost* corresponds to *Shavuot,* which is the festival for which the Jews had gathered to Jerusalem, which corresponds to the day on which the Lord gave Moses the *law* on Mount Sinai way back in the wilderness.

SORROW WILL TURN TO JOY

In verses 17–18 we are told that the disciples were confused by some of what Jesus had just told them. Why do you suppose that might be true?

What metaphor did Jesus use, in verses 21–22, to help His disciples understand what He was saying about the sorrow and joy that would eventually come to them?

What did He say would happen (or not happen!) to the joy they would feel as a result of all this?

Why do you believe He said, in verse 23, "that in that day" they would ask Him nothing?

Fill in the blanks in the following passage.

> *"Until now you have ________ ________ in My name. ________, and you will ________, that your ________ may be full." (John 16:24 NKJV)*

In verse 25, what kind of language did He say He had spoken to them in, to this point?

How did He say this would change, at a later time? What was that time?

Fill in the blanks in the passage below.

> *Jesus answered them, "Do you now believe? Indeed the hour is coming, yes, has now come, that you will be ________ each to his own, and will leave Me alone. And yet I am not ________, because the Father is with Me. These things I have spoken to you, that in Me you may have ________. In the world you will have tribulation; but be of good cheer, I have ________ the world." (John 16:31–33 NKJV)*

John Chapter 17

The text of John 17 is the prayer with which Jesus brought the Last Supper teachings to a close. It has been called the "Lord's high priestly prayer" and even the "Lord's Prayer," although the text of Matthew 6:9–13 is probably more commonly known by the latter name.

In this prayer, after ending His teaching with His triumphant "I have overcome the world" statement, Jesus prayed first for Himself, then for His disciples, and then for all future believers. Read the text of chapter 17 and answer the following questions.

JESUS PRAYS FOR HIMSELF

In verse 1, who did Jesus ask God to glorify, that God Himself might be glorified?

Jesus

Over what did Jesus say that God had given Him authority, in verse 2?

all people

What did He define as "eternal life," in verse 3?

knowing God

What two things did Jesus say that He had done, with respect to the Father, in verse 4?

1. brought Him glory on earth

2. completed His work – teaching, healing, role model, loving

Jesus Prays for His Disciples

From where did Christ say (v. 7) that all things given to Him had come? To whom had He made these things known?

from God as a gift

the disciples

In verse 8, what did He say He had given to the disciples?

God's words

Jesus said, in verse 9, that He did not pray for the world, but for whom?

the disciples

What did He mean, in verse 11, when He said that He was no longer "in the world"? What coming event was He referring to?

preparing for crucifixion

Who did Jesus say, of those whom the Father had given Him, had been lost? What is the common name by which we know this person?

Judas

Why did He say that this person had been lost?

So the scripture would be fulfilled

What did Jesus pray that the Father would do (two things) on behalf of the disciples, in verse 15?

1. dont take them out of the world - let them fulfill their work

2. protect them from Satan

What else did He ask God to do for them, in verse 17?

sanctify them - to make them holy, set apart for sacred use

For whose sake did He say that He sanctified Himself, in verse 19?

the disciples

Jesus Prays for All Believers

In verse 20, Christ began praying for others besides Himself and His disciples. How did He identify these people?

for future believers

What did Jesus indicate was the threefold reason, in verse 21, for which He prayed "for those who will believe in Me through their word" in verse 20?

1. unity

2. they be in God & Jesus

3. Belief world throughout world

Fill in the blanks in the passage below.

> *"And the __________ which You gave Me I have given them, that they may be one just as We are one: I in them, and You in Me; that they may be made __________ in one, and that the world may know that You have sent Me, and have loved them as You have loved Me. Father, I __________ that they also whom You gave Me may be with Me where I am, that they may behold My __________ which You have given Me; for You loved Me before the __________ of the world. O __________ Father! The world has not known You, but I have known You; and these have known that You sent Me. And I have __________ to them Your name, and will declare it, that the __________ with which You loved Me may be in them, and I in them." (John 17:22–26 NKJV)*

PULLING IT ALL TOGETHER . . .

- This section of John, which concludes Jesus' teachings at the Last Supper, begins with what many consider one of the greatest commands in all the Bible, as spoken by Jesus: "That ye love one another." In the same discourse He also said, "Greater love has no one than this, than to lay down one's life for his friends."

- Jesus followed the above with another extremely familiar commentary, explaining that: "If the world hates you, you know that it hated Me before it hated you."

- Next, Jesus promised to send the *Helper* (Holy Spirit) once He Himself had ascended to heaven. He further explained that this would be to the disciples' advantage, for the Helper would be with them at all times, not only to support them but to convict the world of sin, of righteousness, and of judgment.

- This same Spirit of Truth would be constantly available to guide the disciples (and, by extension, all men and women) into all truth.

- Jesus then prayed a lengthy prayer: first, for Himself; then for His disciples; then for all the world.

6 Arrest and Trial

John 18:1–19:16

Before We Begin . . .

What do you believe is the significance of the thirty pieces of silver Judas was paid for betraying Christ? Where else is "thirty pieces of silver" mentioned in the Bible?

In this section of the book of John, as soon as Jesus ended His final words of preparation for His disciples, they left the Upper Room in which they had celebrated the Last Supper (Feast of Passover). They walked across the Kidron Valley, which lay to the east. The Kidron Valley begins at a point just north of Jerusalem; it lies between the temple mount and the Mount of Olives, and eventually ends at the Dead Sea.

In 2 Samuel 15:23–31, we are told the story of David and his flight from Jerusalem to avoid the armies of his own son, Absalom. The same story includes David's betrayal by his friend Ahithophel, even as he, too, crossed the Kidron on his way to the Mount of Olives. How ironic that Christ Himself should soon face betrayal by one of His own in almost the same place.

The Garden to which John referred, known in the other Gospels as the *Garden of Gethsemane*, was an olive grove to which Jesus and His disciples came each night when they were in Jerusalem. During the Feast of the Passover (and during other festival times as well), Jerusalem would literally overflow with thousands of Jews from the surrounding countryside, and a large percentage would wind up sleeping in tents and other temporary shelters.

Read chapter 18 and answer the following questions.

JOHN CHAPTER 18

BETRAYAL AND ARREST IN GETHSEMANE

In verse 1, why do you suppose John did not specifically identify the Garden of Gethsemane by name?

How did Judas know that Jesus and the other disciples would be there that night?

In verse 3, we are told that Judas came with "a detachment of troops, and officers from the chief priests and Pharisees," who "came there with lanterns, torches, and weapons." Why? Was there anything in the life of Jesus Himself that would suggest a need for all this? Was He not, Himself, the very epitome of peace, and should it not have been clear to Judas by then that Christ Himself would not initiate any physical resistance?

Judas and the Thirty Pieces of Silver

In ancient Jewish culture, if a man's wife were convicted of adultery, the husband had three choices:

- First, he could let her pay the price for her own sin, which was death by stoning.
- Second, he could pay the price on her behalf, by giving up his own life.
- Third, he could pay the standard "bride price," which was thirty pieces (shekels) of silver. This would redeem his wife and (in legal terms, at least) reconcile her to her husband (as Hosea was also commanded to do by God, in the book of *Hosea,* as an extended metaphor for God's faithfulness to His people). But this act of mercy and love would also cancel out any future possibility of divorce. Thus, once a man paid the price and redeemed his wife even one time, he was legally bound to her as long as they both lived.

Compare these customs to the story of Jesus Christ and His crucifixion. Who got paid thirty pieces of silver? For what? What did he then do with them once he realized his own sin? And, who gave up His life for an "unfaithful bride"?

In verses 5–6, when Jesus confirmed that He was the One they were looking for, we are told that they all "drew back and fell to the ground." Why do you believe this happened?

Why, according to John's explanation in verse 8, did Jesus ask His abductors to take Him and let the others "go their way"?

Who immediately pulled his sword and used it against those who had come for Jesus?

Why is this person's behavior no real surprise, based on what you already know about him?

In Luke 22:50, we are also told that Simon Peter cut off the right ear of the high priest's servant, probably in an attempt to take off the man's head (at which attempt, it may be safe to assume, the man ducked and almost escaped). But more important, Luke tells us that Christ immediately restored the ear and healed the cut, an amazing act of kindness toward an obvious enemy. Why do you believe John left this detail out of his narrative?

What was Jesus' response to Peter's passion, in verse 11? Write in the missing words, below.

"Put ________ ________ ________
________ ________. Shall I not ________
________ ________ ________ ________
________ ________ ________ ________?"
(NKJV)

Besides arresting Him, what does verse 12 tell us that the men who took Jesus prisoner also did to Him?

According to verses 13–14, (1) to whom did they take Jesus first? (2) what was this man's relationship to Caiaphas—and (3) who was Caiaphas?

1.

2.

3.

Peter Denies Jesus for the First Time

Now comes the first of the three well-known denials of Christ by Peter, exactly as Christ Himself had predicted just hours before. As he does in several other places, John gives us details that we do not find elsewhere. For example, he tells us that two disciples followed Jesus after His arrest. One of these two was Simon Peter. The other disciple—who was known to Annas, the father-in-law of the current high priest (Caiaphas) and the former high priest himself, went with Jesus into Annas's courtyard (v. 15). According to verse 16, Peter stood outside the door.

What did the other disciple then do, to bring Peter inside?

Who do you suspect this other disciple might have been? (Hint: In retrospect, who seemed to be in a position to give us unique details about all that followed?)

What did Annas's servant girl (who kept the door) then ask Peter, even as he came in through the door?

What was Peter's response?

According to verse 18, what did Peter then do, for his own comfort, once he got inside?

WHO WERE ANNAS AND CAIAPHAS?

John tells us that the troops who arrested Jesus took Him first to Annas, then to Caiaphas. Why not directly to Caiaphas?

Annas had been appointed by Quirinius, the governor of Syria, as high priest of the Jews, in AD 6. According to Jewish law, this should have been a lifetime position, but the conquering Romans did not like to leave anyone else in authority—however limited that person's power might be under their supervision—for any length of time. Their goal was to make sure that no one else built too strong a power base of his own. Thus they replaced Annas in AD 16, first by one of his sons, then by his son-in-law, Caiaphas, who held that spot in AD 18–36. Caiaphas was later succeeded by four more of Annas's sons, in succession, then by Annas's grandson.

So . . . why did the troops who arrested Jesus take Him to Annas first? Perhaps because Annas remained the power behind the throne, even though he'd been forced to give up his formal position. Only when he'd conducted what amounted to a *preliminary inquiry* was Jesus sent on to Caiaphas, the official high priest at that time.

What did the high priest (Annas) then do, in verse 19?

*What were the points Jesus made in verse 20, that might have been direct, even preemptive answers to any possible charges of sedition (*sedition: *insurrection against lawful authority)?*

What was the second part of Jesus' response, in verse 21? Why do you think He would add this response? Why not simply stand *on what He had already said?*

Why did the officer strike Jesus, in verse 22? What kind of attitude *did he accuse Jesus of having?*

What was Jesus' mild, entirely logical (and even respectful) response, in verse 23?

To whom did Annas then send Jesus, in verse 24?

Coming back to Peter again, what did he say in verse 25?

What did he do one final time, in verse 27?

What "sign" immediately occurred, to remind Peter of what Christ had predicted?

In Pilate's Court

By now Jesus had been taken to Annas, to Caiaphas, and then to the Preaetorium. What was Pilate's first question, in verse 29, when Jesus finally came before him?

Why do you believe those who brought Jesus to Pilate answered as they did, in verse 30, rather than simply repeating their charges? Does their reply not seem almost an affront to Pilate—or, at the very least, extremely disrespectful?

Why do you think Pilate tried to turn Jesus back over to the Jews, for trial by their own law, in verse 31?

Why did they refuse to accept Jesus back for their own trial? That is, what was the result they desired, as indicated in verses 31–32?

WHAT DOES IT MEAN TO BE "LIFTED UP"?

In John 18:31–32, the Jews made the unmistakable admission that their desire was to see Jesus executed. This was their whole purpose for His arrest. But they had a small legal problem—as a *conquered nation* ruled by Rome, they were not allowed to carry out executions on their own authority. Therefore they had to work things out so that the Romans would do the actual deed *for* them . . . and the Roman method of execution was crucifixion, exactly as Jesus acknowledged when He spoke earlier about being *lifted up*. This was a Hebrew idiom for the custom whereby the Romans executed people by "lifting them up" on a cross to hang until they died.

What did Pilate ask Jesus, in verse 33?

Why do you think Jesus answered as He did, in verse 34? What point was He trying to make, and was that "point" intended only for Pilate or for the entire world to recognize?

Fill in the blanks in the following passage.

> *Pilate answered, "Am I a __________? Your own __________ and the chief priests have delivered You to me. What have You done?"*

Jesus answered, "My __________ is not of this world. If My __________ were of this world, My __________ would fight, so that I should not be __________ to the Jews; but now My kingdom is not from here." Pilate therefore said to Him, "Are You a __________ then?" Jesus answered, "You say rightly that I am a king. For this __________ I was born, and for this cause I have come into the world, that I should bear __________ to the truth. Everyone who is of the __________ hears My voice." Pilate said to Him, "What is __________?" And when he had said this, he went out again to the Jews, and said to them, "I find no __________ in Him at all. (John 18:35–38 NKJV)

What was the name of the man the Jews agreed to release instead of Jesus, in verses 39–40?

John Chapter 19

Preparations for the Crucifixion

John gives us an especially clear picture of Pilate's reluctance to crucify Jesus. He was the only one who had the actual authority, but he did not want to use it. Nonetheless, as chapter 19 shows, the Jews were adamant and Pilate eventually gave them what they wanted.

Read the entire chapter and answer the following questions.

In verse 1 we are told that Pilate "scourged" Jesus. What does this mean?

Why the crown of thorns and the purple robe, of verse 2? What did these symbolize, as further shown by the soldiers' mocking of Jesus in verse 3?

What did Pilate do and say in verse 4? Why do you think he did this?

What did the chief priests and officers of the Jews specifically ask for, in verse 6?

One more time, what did Pilate say in response, in verse 6?

Why did the Jews still insist that Christ should die, in verse 7?

In verses 8–12, Pilate continued to resist the idea of executing Jesus. What was apparently the "clincher," the final argument, spoken to Pilate in verse 12?

In the above exchange, Pilate finally wasted his last opportunity to do the right thing. He seemed to be affected by Jesus' silence, saying in John 19:10: "Do You not know that I have power to crucify You, and power to release You?" (NKJV) Jesus answered to the contrary, of course, in these immortal words:

> *Jesus answered, "You could have no power at all against Me unless it had been given you from above. Therefore the one who delivered Me to you has the greater sin." (John 19:11 NKJV)*

Finally, as we are told in verse 13, Pilate had had enough. What was his last question, as recorded by John in verse 15?

What was the response of the chief priests, also in verse 15, which seems to us an obvious blasphemy all by itself but simply was not recognized as such by them, at that moment in history?

And finally, what was the result as detailed in verse 16?

PULLING IT ALL TOGETHER . . .

- After the Passover meal and His final teachings, Jesus and His disciples walked to an olive grove. John does not identify this grove by name, but it was called the *Garden of Gethsemane* in the Gospels of Matthew and Mark. There, He was betrayed by Judas and taken into custody by a detachment of troops and officers sent by the chief priests and Pharisees.

- Peter, following at a distance, soon had ample opportunity to deny that he was a disciple of Jesus three separate times, before the first rooster crowed that morning, as predicted earlier by Jesus Himself.

- Both Annas (the former high priest) and Caiaphas (the current high priest) were united in their determination to have Jesus executed. Thus He was turned over to the Roman authorities.

- Jesus was bound, beaten, mocked, and ridiculed by the Roman soldiers.

- Pilate did not seem to want to execute Jesus. Indeed, at one point in particular he seemed quite fearful of doing so. But eventually he agreed to do what the Jews could not legally do on their own; that is, to execute Jesus Christ by crucifixion.

7 Crucifixion and Resurrection

John 19:17–20:10

Before We Begin . . .

What is the single most memorable fact about (or aspect of) the Crucifixion, that sticks in your mind?

What aspect of Jesus' behavior during this time of intense suffering do you find most remarkable? (Perhaps it is His courage, His ability to bear pain, or His last-minute thoughts about His mother's welfare and His request that John take care of her.)

This section of John, chapter 19, uses such spare, stark language, it's almost possible to overlook the horrible agony of the death by crucifixion that Jesus Christ endured. On the other hand, much has been written to fill in the details and give us a more accurate picture. Crucifixion, of course, was not a "Jewish" form of execution at all; rather, it was used by the Romans as a means of maximizing the victim's anguish. Its barbaric cruelty also served as a graphic warning to others that death at the hands of the Romans would be anything but quick and painless—and thus should be avoided at all costs.

That Jesus chose to endure it, knowing full well what He was in for—and that He could have refused—simply makes His passion all the more astonishing and compelling.

JOHN CHAPTER 19, CONTINUED . . .

THE KING ON A CROSS

We begin with John 19:17. Read the remainder of chapter 19 and answer the questions that follow.

What was the common name of the place of execution for Jesus?

What was its Hebrew name?

What does verse 17 tell us Jesus carried to that place?

How many others did the Romans crucify along with Him? And, what was His position in the lineup?

What was the wording of the sign Pilate put on the cross with Jesus?

__________ __________ __________, __________

__________ __________ __________ __________.

In what three languages was the sign written? Why not just one?

About That Sign . . .

With respect to the sign saying *"Jesus of Nazareth, the King of the Jews"* that was put over Jesus' head on the cross, John 19:20 tells us: "Then many of the Jews read this title, for the place where Jesus was crucified was near the city; and it was written in *Hebrew, Greek,* and *Latin*" (NKJV, italics added).

Of six popular English translations of the Bible, three more (for a total of four) agree with the above translation, taken from The New King James Version. These include the American Standard Version, The Amplified Bible, and the New American Standard Bible. On the other hand, the New International Version and the English Standard Version say that the sign was written in Aramaic, Greek, and Latin. Why the difference?

This relatively minor discrepancy represents a long, ongoing discussion over what really was the "common" language among the Jews of Jesus' time. The generally accepted answer has been *"Aramaic"* for many years, but recent archaeological evidence at least suggests that *classical Hebrew,* and not Aramaic (a Semitic dialect), might be an equally plausible response. The translations mentioned above (and many others on the market) do not categorically resolve the issue either way, but those that do use the word "Hebrew" can certainly be said to "give hope" to those who believe Hebrew would be the right answer to the question. Either way, it remains a fascinating and inviting mystery, with stout adherents on both sides.

Why do you think the chief priests of the Jews objected to Pilate's sign? What did they want it to say instead—and why? What were they afraid of?

Why do you believe Pilate answered as he did, in verse 22?

From a modern perspective, perhaps, it seems almost strange that the soldiers would consider Jesus' clothes *valuable* enough, in verses 23–24, to divide among themselves. But all clothes in that era were made by hand and were therefore far more expensive, in comparative terms, than the mass-manufactured clothes of today. Doubtless, the cloth in the garments that were divided into four parts (probably Jesus' loose-fitting outer robe) was used for something else, while the seamless inner tunic (an undergarment) could not be so easily divided. The Scripture John quotes, which the soldiers fulfilled by casting lots, was Psalm 22:18.

In verse 26, who do you believe John meant by "the disciple whom He loved"?

How many women were standing by the cross?

Why was John the only disciple mentioned?

IT IS FINISHED

Fill in the blanks in the passage below, which details Jesus' last moments of earthly life.

> *After this, Jesus, knowing that all things were now __________, that the Scripture might be __________, said, "I __________!" Now a vessel full of sour wine was sitting there; and they filled a sponge with sour wine, put it on __________, and put it to His __________. So when Jesus had received the sour wine, He said, "It is __________!" And __________ His head, He gave up His __________. (John 19:28–30 NKJV)*

Verse 31 speaks of "Preparation Day." Preparation Day for what?

The legs of the men who died on the other two crosses were broken, so that they could no longer "push up" with their legs, thus lifting their chests and allowing themselves to continue breathing. But this was not done for Jesus. Why?

Fulfilling Old Testament Prophecies

Aspect of Jesus' Death from the Gospel of John	Old Testament Reference
In obedience to His Father (18:11)	Psalm 40:8
Announced by Himself (18:32; see 3:14)	Numbers 21:8–9
In the place of His people (18:14)	Isaiah 53:4–6
With evildoers (19:18)	Isaiah 53:12
In innocence (19:6)	Isaiah 53:9
Crucified (19:18)	Isaiah 22:16
Buried in a rich man's tomb (19:38–42)	Isaiah 53:9

Jesus Buried in Joseph's Tomb

Why do you think that Joseph of Arimathea was fearful of taking possession of Jesus' body in a public way?

Who also came along, in verse 39, and helped him remove the body of Jesus from the cross?

What was the hundred-pound mixture of myrrh and aloes, brought by this person, to be used for?

John Chapter 20

The Empty Tomb

John 20:1–9 tells how Jesus' resurrection was discovered, early Sunday morning. Read these verses and answer the following questions.

Who was the first person to arrive at the tomb?

What was the first thing she saw?

Who was the first person who actually went into the tomb?

What did he find inside?

What does verse 9 tell us that Peter and John (for John was the "other disciple" of these verses) did not yet understand?

The Role of Women in the Life of Jesus

John 19:25 lists three women who "stood by the cross" of Jesus—His mother, His mother's sister, Mary (the wife of Clopas), and Mary Magdalene. Of His disciples only John was there at the Crucifixion, to whom Jesus commended the care of His mother. But what the Scriptures make obvious is that, in addition to being there at His death, women played a major part in the life of Jesus. For example, they . . .

nurtured Him as He grew up	Luke 2:51
listened to Him as He taught	Luke 10:39
offered hospitality to Him and His companions	Mark 1:29–31
were featured in His parables	Matthew 13:33; 24:41
traveled with Him and helped finance His ministry	Luke 8:1–3
proclaimed that He was the Messiah	John 4:28–30
were treated by Him with respect and compassion	John 4:5–27; 11:32–33
were healed by Him	Matthew 9:20–22; Luke 13:10–17
were praised by Him for their faith	Mark 7:24–30
were commended by Him for their generosity	Mark 12:41–44
worshiped Him and prepared His body for burial	Matthew 26:6–13
stood by Him at the cross	Matthew 27:55; John 19:25
assisted in His burial	Mark 16:1; Luke 23:55–24:1
first saw Him after He'd been resurrected	John 20:16
went to tell the rest of His followers that He had risen	John 20:18

Pulling It All Together . . .

- Jesus was executed by Roman soldiers, acting on Pilate's order. He was crucified on a wooden cross, set between two others on a hill at a place called Golgotha, just outside Jerusalem.

- Pilate had his soldiers place a sign above Jesus' head on the cross, written in three languages and reading: "Jesus of Nazareth, the King of the Jews." This was Pilate's "last laugh," for the Jewish leaders who had called for Jesus' death certainly did not want Him known as the *King of the Jews.*

- Unlike those of the two men who were crucified at the same time, Jesus' legs were not broken; fulfilling prophecies that stated none of the Messiah's bones would be broken.

- Jesus was taken down by Joseph of Arimathea, assisted by Nicodemus. Together they wrapped Jesus' body in linen strips, heavily spiced with the myrrh and aloes Nicodemus had brought along for that purpose. These were costly spices. On the other hand, the entire process by which these two men cared for the body of Jesus could have been extremely costly for both of them, had the leaders of the Jews known what they were doing and taken exception to it.

- Early Sunday morning, Mary Magdalene discovered that Jesus' tomb was open. She ran to tell Peter and John, who then raced each other to the tomb!

- Peter went inside first and discovered that Christ was gone, and only the linens used to wrap His body had been left behind. John came in next, and together the two realized that Christ had, indeed, risen from the dead—exactly as promised in Scriptures with which they were not yet familiar.

8 Final Appearances

John 20:11–31

Before We Begin . . .

At this point, why do you think John wrote his own Gospel, if it contains much of the same information as the Gospels of Matthew, Mark, and Luke?

This section of John's Gospel begins with one of the more poignant scenes in the Bible. Mary Magdalene has come to the tomb, early in the morning on the first day of the week. Jesus had been laid in the tomb on Friday; had lain there on Saturday (which was known as *Shabbat*, an especially holy Jewish Sabbath because it was also the Passover Sabbath), and now it was Sunday morning.

Ancient Burial Customs

The Holy Land was (and still is) a desert country of extreme dryness and heat, especially in the summer. But, unlike the Egyptians, the Jewish people of that time did not embalm the bodies of their dead. Thus they buried them as quickly as possible, often (as with Jesus) on the very day they died, because physical bodies decomposed rapidly in the dry heat of the desert.

Both Joseph of Arimathea and Nathanael were following the burial customs of their time—Joseph by removing Jesus' body from the cross and laying it in a tomb within hours of His death; Nathanael by providing spices and linens with which to anoint and wrap His body. The spices were intended to counteract the scent of death that would soon follow; they were often applied as an act of love, a final show of respect and goodwill toward the deceased. This was abundantly true in the case of Jesus Christ.

John did not give us a specific reason for Mary's visit other than the obvious—that Mary almost certainly would have come, with other women as we are told in other Gospels, to worship Christ and, perhaps, simply to be near Him. The Gospel of Luke tells us that Mary—and other women who came with her—had brought spices, undoubtedly to anoint Jesus' body. However, John also tells us that Nathanael and Joseph of Arimathea had already done so.

In any case, Mary soon found herself standing face-to-face and speaking with Christ Himself—risen from the dead and alive!

JOHN CHAPTER 20, CONTINUED . . .

MARY MAGDALENE SEES THE RISEN LORD

In verse 11, what was Mary doing as she stood outside the tomb?

What did she see when she looked into the tomb?

What did the angels say to her, in verse 13?

As soon as she responded to them she turned around and saw Jesus standing there. But she didn't recognize Him! Who did she think it was, instead?

What did Jesus say to her when He first spoke, in verse 15?

"Woman, __________ __________ __________ __________? Whom __________ __________ __________?" (NKJV)

What did He finally say to her that caused her to recognize Him?

What is the meaning of the word Rabboni?

Why do you suppose Jesus told Mary not to "cling" to Him? He said He had not yet ascended to His Father, but why would that mean she should not "cling"?

What did Mary Magdalene immediately do?

THE APOSTLES COMMISSIONED

In verse 19, why do you think the disciples were assembled in a room with the doors shut "for fear of the Jews"?

What did Jesus say when He appeared in their midst?

What did He then show them?

Fill in the blanks in the familiar passage below.

> *So Jesus said to them again, "__________ to you! As the __________ has sent Me, I also __________ you." And when He had said this, He __________ on them, and said to them, "__________ the Holy Spirit. If you forgive the sins of any, they are __________ them; if you __________ the sins of any, they are retained." (John 20:21–23 NKJV)*

SEEING AND BELIEVING

In verses 24–25, the disciples told Thomas that they had seen Jesus. What was his immediate response?

Eight days later Jesus appeared to the disciples again, and Thomas was with them this time. What did Jesus then do to dispel Thomas's doubt?

What was Thomas's response?

And what were Jesus' exact "final" words on the subject, spoken directly to Thomas, in verse 29?

> *"Thomas, __________ you have __________ Me, you have __________. Blessed are those who have __________ seen and __________ __________ __________." (NKJV)*

The Purpose of the Book of John—That You May Believe

John did something very unusual in the last two verses of chapter 20. Writing his Gospel was definitely not an intellectual pursuit for him. He was not trying to record history in the same sense, for example, that a well-known contemporary historian such as Josephus was—although Josephus was very selective in his own way, and might even have been influenced by his own *personal* fear of the Romans.

In any case, John was certainly not trying to provide a historic record in the same way that modern history books, complete with thousands of carefully annotated footnotes and years of plodding research, propose to do. On the contrary, John

DOUBTING THOMAS

The "doubting Thomas" phrase has probably been a familiar part of some languages since biblical times. Many times it has been used, in English at least, as a *derogatory* term, as though someone who "doubts" is somehow less "mentally strong" or "faith-blessed" than others.

The truth could well be something else entirely. For example, the man many people consider the greatest servant of God in the Bible, Moses, certainly "doubted" the Lord's plans more than once. Indeed, when he learned that he would not be allowed to enter the Promised Land of Canaan, Moses literally pushed the Lord to the very limit and was essentially told to be quiet and not bring it up again—in no uncertain terms (Deut. 3:23–26 NKJV)!

Moses' relationship with God epitomized the Jewish concept of "darashing," as did similar relationships with God that were had by any number of Old Testament figures—Jacob, David, Jeremiah, and Hosea, to name just a few. A *darash* can be many things, but at its best it's a respectful debate in which two people state differing opinions and then work out their differences. Even Abraham *darashed* with God, over the fate of Sodom and Gomorrah. He didn't win, but God definitely would have given in if Abraham's assumptions had proved true, and there actually had been ten good men in those two towns.

What is the point of all this? Only to say that God does not punish those who ask hard questions. On the contrary, many scholars believe that "Come now, and let us reason together" (Isa. 1:18 NKJV) is a far more accurate characterization of God's attitude toward *darashing*, or *discussing* issues that are hard for us to understand at first.

Thomas is known as a doubter, but perhaps he simply needed a little nudge to see the truth more clearly.

intended for us to think about the *theological significance* of everything he recorded. What was the meaning of the specific miracles, or "signs," that he chose to include? Who was this "Jesus Christ" person? Was He sent directly from the Father, as He Himself said, or was He someone else? At the same time, what about all the signs Jesus did that John did not write about?

John thus brought his book to a close with a stirring proclamation of Jesus' victory over death. Here are the words with which he brought all this together:

> And truly Jesus did many other signs in the presence of His disciples, which are not written in this book; but these are written that you may believe that Jesus is the Christ, the Son of God, and that believing you may have life in His name. (John 20:30–31 NKJV)

Pulling It All Together . . .

- After Peter and John had seen the empty tomb and gone home, Mary remained behind, weeping. Then she saw a man standing there, whom she believed to be the gardener. But it was Jesus! She then went and told the disciples that He had risen and was alive.

- On the evening of the same day, most of the disciples were together in a room, with the doors closed. Suddenly Jesus appeared among them and spoke to them.

- Thomas was not with the other disciples on the above occasion, and he did not truly believe that they had actually seen Christ Himself. Eight days later the disciples were together again, inside, and once again Jesus appeared among them. This time He convinced Thomas that He was really the risen Christ, by showing Thomas His wounds.

- John also tells us that Jesus did many other signs in the presence of His disciples—too many to be included in John's Gospel. But he tells us they were done so that we would have the evidence we need to believe that Jesus Christ was truly the Son of God.

9 EPILOGUE

JOHN 21:1–25

Before We Begin . . .

Do you remember what final miracle Jesus performed for the disciples, after His resurrection? (Hint: This was not included among the seven miracles, or "signs" that John built much of his Gospel around, but was every bit as miraculous as any of the others.)

Even as John made a point of beginning his Gospel with an introduction, he ended it with an epilogue, giving us additional glimpses of Christ after the Resurrection but before He ascended to be with God the Father in heaven. The last chapter begins with Jesus' familiar encounter with the disciples along the shore of the Sea of Tiberius (Galilee), as they return from a night of fishing. And once again, though they were frustrated by their lack of success, He rewards them richly.

JOHN CHAPTER 21

BREAKFAST BY THE SEA

Where did Jesus show Himself to some of the disciples, in verse 1?

What were these disciples doing when they saw Jesus?

What was His first question to them, in verse 5?

What did He then tell them to do?

When they did as He directed, what happened?

What did Peter immediately realize, and what did He do?

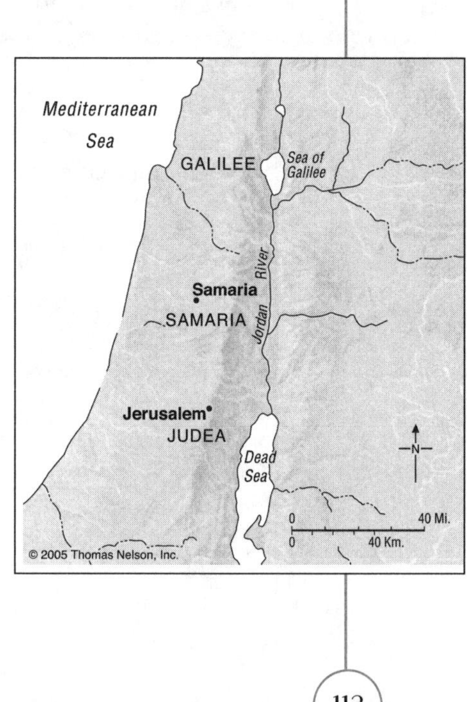

What Was It Like to Be a Fisherman on the Sea of Galilee in Ancient Israel?

This chapter of John provides several clues about what full-time work as a fisherman was like in first-century Israel. Modern scholarship has also helped to fill in quite a few more details. For example:

- Peter and Andrew, and James and John, probably worked in small wooden boats that were no more than eighteen to twenty feet long.
- They used nets that were made of linen, which had to be washed and dried at the end of each day's work or they would rot.
- It required four men to man each boat and handle the nets.
- They fished at night, because their nets would be far too visible to the fish in daylight.
- They often stripped to their bare skin—to no more than a loincloth—because they were constantly getting wet. Indeed, many times they spent the greater part of the night *in the water itself,* despite freezing cold and blowing wind.
- They came to shore each morning, virtually exhausted from the night's work. They slept in the morning—indeed, fishing villages in that era were often like ghost towns until afternoon.

In other words, these were strong, hearty men who were probably too tough to catch a common cold! And Jesus Himself, on more than one occasion, was in their boats with them and probably helped them land their nets.

What did these disciples find when they reached the shore?

How many fish did they catch?

Jesus Restores Peter

John now tells us how Jesus reestablished His relationship with Peter, in what could easily serve as a model for our own behavior in similar situations. Surely Peter must have felt a certain amount of embarrassment and chagrin, although the text does not say so.

What were the three things that Jesus told Peter to do, in verses 15–19, after each affirmation from Peter that he loved Him? (One of these is repeated twice; go to the end of this passage for #3.)

Forgiveness for Peter . . .

Most believers in Christ know that Peter denied Him three times before His crucifixion, as prophesied by Christ Himself. However, the book of John provides a poignant example of genuine forgiveness that, at first glance, might seem a little hard to understand.

The question is, why did Jesus ask Peter three times, after the Resurrection, whether Peter loved Him? Was it just because Peter had denied Him three times, or was there a deeper meaning beyond the "symmetry" of three corresponding affirmations? Most scholars point to the differences in the Greek between the words Jesus used for "love," ranging from "a love of commitment" to "a love of purest and deepest friendship." In addition to extending simple forgiveness, Christ seemed to be doing several things at once. He was reaffirming Peter's commitment to Him, He was restoring Peter's self-confidence, He was banishing his shame, and He was making a clear statement, in front of the other disciples, that Peter had been restored to a position of leadership among them.

What did Jesus also tell Peter, which John explains as "signifying by what death he would glorify God"? What do you think that meant?

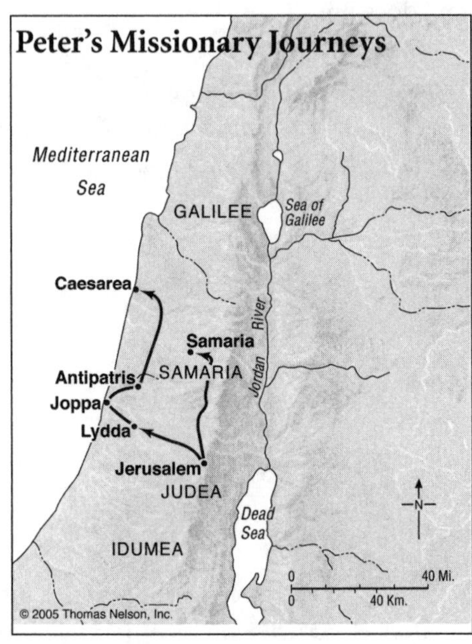

The final section of this Gospel, John 21:20–25, might be called something of a *coda*, or perhaps a *colophon,* as it is more commonly known—meaning "an inscription or an identifying device placed at the very end of the text." A colophon can also be somewhat of a trademark, and certainly we have learned to identify John's references to himself via his trademark phrase, "the disciple whom Jesus loved," as used here in verse 20.

Peter also remained true to his own nature in this last section, inquiring in verse 21 about what would eventually happen to John—now that he had been told his own fate in John 21:18–19. Perhaps only Peter would be so inquisitive, and so ripe for the rebuke that followed. Christ told him in no uncertain terms—as He assuredly would also say to us—that Peter's (our) job was to *follow Him* without being sidetracked or distracted by what someone else might do or might not do.

Predicting Peter's Death

In John 21:18–23, Jesus does something that can seem a bit difficult to understand for many readers. After forgiving Peter three separate times, He tells Peter that, contrary to the freedom he enjoyed when he was younger, later Peter would be arrested, bound, and taken away to be executed.

In verse 19, Jesus then explains that Peter will one day die as a martyr—but that God would give him the courage he would need. Even as he had once denied Christ most vehemently, Peter would one day glorify God with equal zeal.

The Gospel of John ends with the passage below, indicating once again that, no matter how many details from the life of Jesus that John's own book might contain, even when combined with the other three Gospels, it cannot possibly tell the whole story of Jesus' life on Earth.

Here, again, are John's closing words, of which the words "and we know that his testimony is true" might have been added as an endorsement by someone else.

> *This is the disciple who testifies of these things, and wrote these things; and we know that his testimony is true. And there are also many other things that Jesus did, which if they were written one by one, I suppose that even the world itself could not contain the books that would be written. Amen. (John 21:24–25 NKJV)*

Pulling It All Together . . .

- Jesus appeared to some of His disciples for a third and final time before He ascended to heaven. It happened at the seashore—as several of them were returning from a night of fishing (during which they had caught nothing), He was waiting for them on the shore with a fire built and fish cooking in the coals.

- They were frustrated because they had caught nothing, but He told them to lower their nets one more time, on the right side of their boat. When they did so they caught a huge haul of 153 large fish.

- Jesus asked Peter three separate times if he loved Him. Each time Peter answered "Yes." In response, Jesus told him to "Feed My lambs," "Tend My sheep," and "Follow Me."

- Jesus then admonished Peter not to be concerned with what happened to other people, but—again—to concentrate all his attention on following Him.

10 Coming to a Close

As we have long since established, John did not write his Gospel to provide a day-by-day, month-by-month, or even year-by-year biography of Jesus Christ while He lived on Earth. Neither did John intend to give us a detailed chronology—an event-by-event listing of everything that happened during Jesus' thirty-three years of earthly life.

John was *selective* about what he chose to report, and John *made* his selections according to his own very strict and very clear criteria. He stated those criteria in his own words, in different ways, at different places within his Gospel. Perhaps they can be best summarized as follows:

1. John wanted to establish, once and for all, that Jesus Christ *is the Son of God.*

2. He wanted to establish, once and for all, that Jesus Christ, as the divine Son of God, *is the promised Messiah.*

3. He wanted to establish both of the above points—which he considered one and the same—so that the millions of people who would read his words in the centuries after he wrote them down, would have the information they needed to believe in Jesus Christ.

Granted, John could not have known how many people would read his Gospel, for he had no way of comprehending those things that Jesus Himself tells us "only the Father could know" (Matt. 24:36; Mark 13:32 NKJV). But this, of course, was not his concern.

John's concern was to show us how Jesus Christ, in His own words and deeds, truly was and is . . .

- The Bread of Life
- The Light of the World
- The Gate for the sheep
- The Good Shepherd
- The Resurrection and the Life
- The Way and the Truth and the Life
- The True Vine

These things we have mentioned before, but they certainly bear repeating—even as they have been repeated for perhaps millions of times since John wrote them down. This, above all, is the most profound testimony to both the divinity of Christ and the message John proclaimed about Him.

The book of John has changed countless lives. It has shown countless people the truth of Jesus Christ. It has changed hearts, changed nations, and even changed empires.

> *And you shall know the truth, and the truth shall make you free. (John 8:32* NKJV)

How to Build Your Reference Library

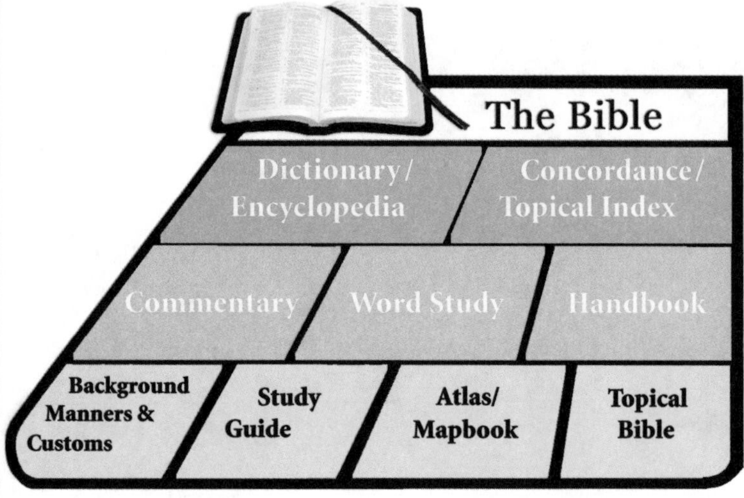

Great Resources for Building Your Reference Library

Dictionaries and Encyclopedias

All About the Bible: The Ultimate A-to-Z® Illustrated Guide to the Key People, Places, and Things

Every Man in the Bible by Larry Richards

Every Woman in the Bible by Larry Richards and Sue Richards

Nelson's Compact Bible Dictionary

Nelson's Illustrated Encyclopedia of the Bible

Nelson's New Illustrated Bible Dictionary

Nelson's Student Bible Dictionary

So That's What It Means! The Ultimate A-to-Z Resource by Don Campbell, Wendell Johnston, John Walvoord, and John Witmer

Vine's Complete Expository Dictionary of Old and New Testament Words by W. E. Vine and Merrill F. Unger

Concordances and Topical Indexes

Nelson's Quick Reference Bible Concordance by Ronald F. Youngblood

The New Strong's Exhaustive Concordance of the Bible by James Strong

Commentaries

Believer's Bible Commentary by William MacDonald

Matthew Henry's Concise Commentary on the Whole Bible by Matthew Henry

The MacArthur Bible Commentary by John MacArthur

Nelson's New Illustrated Bible Commentary

Thru the Bible series by J. Vernon McGee

Handbooks

Nelson's Compact Bible Handbook

Nelson's Complete Book of Bible Maps and Charts

Nelson's Illustrated Bible Handbook

Nelson's New Illustrated Bible Manners and Customs by Howard F. Vos

With the Word: The Chapter-by-Chapter Bible Handbook by Warren W. Wiersbe

For more great resources, please visit *www.thomasnelson.com.*